CROATIA TRAVEL GUIDE 2023:

The Beginner's Guide For Planning Your Trip To Croatia, With Slovenia And Montenegro

Natalie R. Pate

Table Of Contents

CHAPTER 8: ADDITIONAL RESOURCES

AND INFORMATION.................................227

CHAPTER 1: INTRODUCTION TO CROATIA

As I stepped off the plane and onto Croatian soil, I was immediately struck by the warm, Mediterranean air. I had always dreamed of visiting Croatia, and now that dream was finally becoming a reality.

After collecting my luggage and making my way through customs, I hopped into a taxi and headed for my hotel in the heart of Dubrovnik. As we drove through the winding streets, I couldn't help but marvel at the stunning views of the Adriatic Sea and the ancient walls that encircled the city.

Upon arriving at my hotel, I was welcomed by the friendly staff and shown to my room, which had a balcony overlooking the old town. After freshening up and unpacking, I headed out to explore the city.

As I walked the narrow streets lined with charming cobblestone alleyways and colorful houses, I couldn't help but feel a sense of awe at the rich history that surrounded me. Everywhere I looked, there were reminders of Dubrovnik's storied past - from the ancient churches and monasteries to the stunning fortifications that guarded the city's gates.

I spent the next few days exploring Dubrovnik and its surroundings, taking in the sights and sounds of this beautiful city. I visited the stunning island of

Mljet, hiked through the breathtaking Plitvice Lakes National Park, and even took a boat tour to the Elaphiti Islands.

As my visit came to an end, I knew that I would always cherish the memories of my time in Croatia. From the breathtaking landscapes and rich history to the warm and welcoming people, there was no place I would rather have been.

One of my favorite experiences during my visit to Croatia was touring the old town of Dubrovnik. As I walked along the ancient walls that encircled the city, I couldn't help but feel a sense of awe at the rich history that surrounded me. The walls, which date back to the Middle Ages, are a testament to Dubrovnik's past as a powerful maritime republic.

As I walked along the walls, I marveled at the stunning views of the Adriatic Sea and the surrounding countryside. I could see for miles in every direction, and the views were simply breathtaking.

After touring the walls, I made my way to the city's main square, the Placa. Here, I was surrounded by charming cobblestone streets, colorful houses, and ancient churches and monasteries. I spent hours exploring the narrow streets, marveling at the city's rich history and soaking up the local culture.

But my visit to Dubrovnik wasn't just about exploring the city. I also took the opportunity to venture out into the surrounding countryside and explore some of Croatia's other breathtaking destinations. I visited the stunning island of Mljet, hiked through the breathtaking Plitvice Lakes National Park, and even took a boat tour to the Elaphiti Islands.

No matter where I went, I was struck by the beauty and history of Croatia. From the ancient cities to the breathtaking landscapes, this country has something for everyone. And I knew that I would always cherish the memories of my time in this magical place.

Overview Of The Country

Croatia is a country located in the southeastern part of Europe, on the Balkan Peninsula. It is bordered by Slovenia to the northwest, Hungary to the northeast, Serbia to the east, Bosnia and Herzegovina to the southeast, and Montenegro to the south. The country has a long and fascinating history, with roots that can be traced back to ancient Roman times.

One of the most striking features of Croatia is its stunning natural beauty. The country is home to a diverse range of landscapes, from the picturesque Adriatic coast, with its crystal clear waters and sandy beaches, to the stunning national parks and forests that cover much of the interior.

One of the most popular tourist destinations in Croatia is the city of Dubrovnik, which is located on the southern coast of the country. Dubrovnik is a stunning city with a rich history and a stunning old town that is surrounded by ancient walls. The city is also home to several charming squares and narrow streets lined with colorful houses, churches, and monasteries.

In addition to Dubrovnik, Croatia is home to several other beautiful cities, including Split, which is located on the central coast and is known for its ancient Roman ruins and charming old town. Zagreb, the capital of Croatia, is another popular destination, with a vibrant culture and several interesting museums and galleries.

Croatia is also home to several stunning national parks and forests, including Plitvice Lakes National Park, which is home to a series of stunning waterfalls and lakes. The country is also home to several beautiful islands, including the Elaphiti Islands and the island of Mljet, which are popular with tourists who are looking for a more relaxed and secluded getaway.

Croatia is a stunning country with a rich history and a diverse range of landscapes and attractions. Whether you're looking for a relaxing beach vacation, a cultural city break, or an adventure in the great outdoors, Croatia has something to offer everyone.

Geography And Climate

The country has a long and fascinating history, with roots that can be traced back to ancient Roman times.

One of the most striking features of Croatia is its stunning natural beauty. The country is home to a diverse range of landscapes, from the picturesque Adriatic coast, with its crystal clear waters and sandy beaches, to the stunning national parks and forests that cover much of the interior.

One of the most popular tourist destinations in Croatia is the city of Dubrovnik, which is located on the southern coast of the country. Dubrovnik is a stunning city with a rich history and a stunning old town that is surrounded by ancient walls. The city is also home to several charming squares and narrow streets lined with colorful houses, churches, and monasteries.

In addition to Dubrovnik, Croatia is home to several other beautiful cities, including Split, which is located on the central coast and is known for its ancient Roman ruins and charming old town. Zagreb, the capital of Croatia, is another popular destination, with a vibrant culture and several interesting museums and galleries.

Croatia is also home to several stunning national parks and forests, including Plitvice Lakes National Park, which is home to a series of stunning waterfalls and lakes. The country is also home to several beautiful islands, including the Elaphiti Islands and the island of Mljet, which are popular with tourists who are looking for a more relaxed and secluded getaway.

Croatia is a stunning country with a rich history and a diverse range of landscapes and attractions. Whether you're looking for a relaxing beach vacation, a cultural city break, or an adventure in the great outdoors, Croatia has something to offer everyone.

Language And Culture

Croatia is a country with a rich cultural heritage, and this is reflected in the language and traditions of its people. The official language of Croatia is Croatian, which is a South Slavic language that is closely related to Serbian, Bosnian, and Montenegrin. Croatian is spoken by the majority of the population and is used in all official and public settings, including schools and the media.

Croatian culture is heavily influenced by its history and location in the Balkans. The country has a long and varied history, and this is reflected in its art, literature, music, and architecture. Croatia is home to several beautiful churches, monasteries, and castles, as well as several museums and galleries that showcase the country's rich cultural heritage.

Croatian cuisine is also an important aspect of the country's culture, and it is heavily influenced by Mediterranean, Central European, and Eastern European flavors. Croatian dishes often include a variety of meats, vegetables, and grains, and are often served with local cheeses, bread, and wines.

In addition to its cultural traditions, Croatia is also home to several festivals and events that celebrate the country's history and culture. The most famous of these is the Dubrovnik Summer Festival, which is held annually in the city of Dubrovnik and features a range of cultural events, including music, theater, and dance performances.

Croatian culture is a unique blend of old and new, and it is this diversity that makes it such a fascinating and rich cultural experience. Whether you're exploring the country's ancient cities, enjoying its delicious cuisine, or taking part in its vibrant cultural events, there is always something new and exciting to discover in Croatia.

Best Times To Visit

Croatia is a beautiful country with a lot to offer, and the best time to visit depends on your interests and preferences. Here are some factors to consider when deciding when to visit Croatia:

Weather: Croatia has a Mediterranean climate, which means it experiences hot, dry summers and mild, wet winters. The summer months of June to August are the busiest and most popular times to visit, with temperatures ranging from the mid-70s to mid-80s Fahrenheit. If you prefer cooler weather, the spring and fall months of April to May and September to October are generally pleasant, with temperatures ranging from the mid-50s to mid-70s Fahrenheit.

Crowds: As mentioned, the summer months are the busiest and most crowded time to visit Croatia. If you prefer a more peaceful and relaxing vacation, you may want to consider visiting during the shoulder seasons of spring or fall.

Festivals and events: Croatia is home to several festivals and events throughout the year, and if you're interested in experiencing local culture, you may want to plan your visit around one of these events. For example, the Dubrovnik Summer Festival is held in July and August and features a range of cultural events, including music, theater, and dance performances.

Beach season: Croatia's Adriatic coast is home to several stunning beaches, and the beach season runs from May to September. If you're looking to spend your vacation lounging on the beach, you'll want to visit during these months.

Pricing: Prices for accommodations and activities in Croatia tend to be highest during the summer months when demand is highest. If you're looking to save money on your vacation, you may want to consider visiting during the shoulder seasons or in the off-season.

Water activities: If you're planning to go swimming, boating, or diving during your visit to Croatia, you'll want to visit during the summer months when the water is warmest. The water temperature in the Adriatic Sea ranges from the mid-60s to mid-70s Fahrenheit from May to September.

Cultural events: In addition to the Dubrovnik Summer Festival, Croatia is home to several other cultural events throughout the year. For example, the Pula Film Festival is held in July and features a range of international and Croatian films, and the Split Film Festival is held in September and showcases a variety of films from around the world.

Skiing: If you're interested in skiing, you'll want to visit Croatia during the winter months when the ski resorts are open. The ski season in Croatia typically runs from December to April, depending on the weather conditions.

Overall, the best time to visit Croatia depends on your interests and preferences. No matter when you visit, you're sure to have a memorable and enjoyable vacation experience.

CHAPTER 2: PLANNING YOUR TRIP

Planning a trip to Croatia can be an exciting and rewarding experience. With its stunning natural beauty, rich cultural heritage, and friendly locals, Croatia is a destination that is sure to leave a lasting impression. Here are some tips to help you plan your trip to Croatia:

- **Decide when to visit:** As mentioned, the best time to visit Croatia depends on your interests and preferences. Consider factors such as the weather, crowds, festivals and events, beach season, and pricing when deciding when to visit.

- **Book your flights and accommodations:** Once you've decided when to visit, it's time to book your flights and accommodations. There are several airports in Croatia, including in the cities of Dubrovnik, Split, and Zagreb, so you'll want to choose the airport that is most convenient for your travel plans. There are also a variety of accommodations available in Croatia, including hotels, guesthouses, apartments, and villas. Consider your budget and what type of experience you're looking for when selecting your accommodations.

- **Research your destination:** Croatia is a diverse country with a lot to offer, and it's a good idea to do some research before your trip to help you plan your itinerary. Consider what type of activities you're interested in, such as sightseeing, hiking, beach-going, or skiing, and make a list of the places you want to visit and things you want to do.

- **Get travel insurance:** Travel insurance is always a good idea, especially when traveling to a foreign country. It can protect you in the event of unexpected emergencies, such as flight cancellations, medical issues, or lost luggage.

- **Learn some basic Croatian phrases:** While many Croatians speak English, it's always helpful to learn a few basic phrases in Croatian to show your appreciation for the local culture.

Some useful phrases to know include "hello" (dobar dan), "please" (molim), and "thank you" (hvala).

planning a trip to Croatia requires some preparation, but with a little planning and research, you can have a smooth and enjoyable vacation experience.

Visa Requirements

allows citizens of certain countries to enter the country without a visa for stays of up to 90 days. If you are a citizen of an EU or Schengen member country, you do not need a visa to enter Croatia.

If you are a citizen of a non-EU/Schengen country, you may need a visa to enter Croatia, depending on the purpose and duration of your stay. If you are planning to visit Croatia for tourism, business, or other short-term stays, you may be eligible for a short-stay visa, also known as a Schengen visa. If you are planning to stay in Croatia for a longer period, you may need to apply for a long-stay visa.

To apply for a visa to Croatia, you will need to submit a completed application form, a valid passport, two recent passport-sized photographs, proof of sufficient funds to cover your stay, and documentation supporting the purpose of your trip. You may also need to provide additional documents, depending on the purpose of your visit.

It is important to note that the visa requirements for Croatia may change, so it is always a good idea to check with the Croatian embassy or consulate in your home country before planning your trip. You can find more information about visa requirements for Croatia on the website of the Croatian Ministry of Foreign and European Affairs.

To apply for a long-stay visa, you will need to submit a completed application form, a valid passport, two recent passport-sized photographs, proof of sufficient funds to cover your stay, and documentation supporting the purpose of your trip. You may also need to provide additional documents, such as a letter of invitation from a Croatian employer or a letter of acceptance from a Croatian educational institution.

Once you have submitted your application and all required documents, the Croatian embassy or consulate will review your application and decide whether to grant you a long-stay visa. If your application is approved, you will be issued a visa sticker that will be placed on your passport. You will need to present this visa sticker when you enter Croatia.

If you are planning to stay in Croatia for a long time, it is important to apply for a long-stay visa well in advance of your trip. The process of applying for a long-stay visa can be lengthy, and you will want to ensure that you have enough time to complete all the necessary steps before your trip.

In addition to applying for a long-stay visa, you may also need to apply for a residence permit if you are planning to stay in Croatia for more than 90 days. A residence permit is a document that allows you to legally reside in Croatia for a specific time. You can apply for a residence permit at the Croatian Ministry of the Interior after you arrive in the country.

If you are planning to visit Croatia for work or study, it is important to research the visa and residence permit requirements and to apply for these documents well in advance of your trip. This will ensure that you have all the necessary documents to enter and reside in the country legally.

Transportation Options

There are several transportation options available for getting to and around Croatia. Here are some of the most popular options:

Air travel: The main international airport in Croatia is Zagreb Airport, which is located in the capital city of Zagreb. There are also international airports in the cities of Dubrovnik, Split, and Pula. Many major international airlines operate flights to Croatia, and several low-cost carriers offer flights to the country.

Bus travel: There are regular bus services that connect Croatia to several European countries, including Austria, Germany, Italy, and Slovenia. Bus travel can be an affordable and convenient way to get to Croatia, and many of the buses are modern and comfortable.

Train travel: Croatia is connected to several European countries by rail, and there are regular trains that operate between Croatia and countries such as Austria, Hungary, and Slovenia. Train travel can be a comfortable and scenic way to get to Croatia, and there are several train classes available to suit different budgets.

Car travel: If you prefer to travel by car, you can drive to Croatia from several European countries. Croatia has a well-developed network of roads, and driving is generally a safe and convenient way to get

around the country. You will need to have a valid driver's license and an International Driving Permit if you are driving in Croatia.

Boat travel: Croatia is home to several stunning islands, and many tourists choose to visit the country by boat. Several ferries operate between the Croatian mainland and the islands, and you can also take a boat tour to explore the coastline and islands.

Overall, there are several transportation options available for getting to and around Croatia, and the best option for you will depend on your budget and preferences. No matter how you choose to travel, Croatia is a beautiful and welcoming country that is sure to provide a memorable vacation experience.

Money And Currency

Croatia is a member of the European Union (EU) and the currency used in the country is the Croatian kuna (HRK). The kuna is divided into 100 lips, and there are coins in denominations of 1, 2, 5, 10, 20, and 50 lips, as well as 1, 2, and 5 kuna coins. There are also banknotes in denominations of 5, 10, 20, 50, 100, 200, 500, and 1,000 kunas.

The kuna is a stable currency and is pegged to the euro, so you can expect the exchange rate to be similar to that of the euro. You can exchange foreign currency for kuna at banks, currency exchange offices, and some hotels and restaurants. You can also use ATMs to withdraw kuna using a credit or debit card. It is important to note that not all ATMs in Croatia accept all types of cards, so it is a good idea to have a backup option in case your card is not accepted.

Credit cards are widely accepted in Croatia, especially in major cities and tourist areas. Visa and Mastercard are the most widely accepted cards, followed by American Express and Diners Club. It is always a good idea to have some cash on hand, as not all businesses accept credit cards, and you may need cash for smaller purchases or to tip in restaurants and hotels.

The Croatian kuna is a stable and convenient currency, and you should have no problem accessing and using money during your trip to Croatia. Just be sure to have a mix of cash and credit cards to ensure you have a backup option in case one is not accepted

Mobile Phone And Internet Access

Mobile phone and internet access in Croatia are generally reliable and widely available. Here are some things to consider when using your mobile phone and accessing the internet in Croatia:

Mobile phone service: Mobile phone service in Croatia is generally reliable and widely available, especially in major cities and tourist areas. If you have an unlocked phone and a compatible SIM card, you can purchase a prepaid SIM card in Croatia to use during your trip. You can also purchase a SIM card before your trip from an international phone carrier that offers service in Croatia.

Internet access: Internet access in Croatia is widely available, and there are several options for accessing the internet while you are in the country. Many hotels and restaurants offer free Wi-Fi, and you can also purchase a prepaid SIM card that includes data for internet access. If you prefer a more flexible option, you can also purchase a portable Wi-Fi hotspot that allows you to access the internet from any location.

Roaming charges: If you are using your mobile phone from a foreign country, you may incur roaming charges for calls, texts, and data usage. To avoid these charges, you can purchase a local SIM card or turn off roaming on your phone and use a local Wi-Fi network to make calls and access the internet.

International calls: If you need to make international calls from Croatia, you can use a local SIM card with an international calling plan or use a phone card or calling app to make calls at a lower cost.

Mobile phone and internet access in Croatia are generally reliable and widely available, and you should have no problem staying connected during your trip to the country. Just be sure to research your options and consider your usage needs before your trip to ensure you have the best option for your needs.

CHAPTER 3: GETTING AROUND CROATIA

Croatia is a beautiful country located in southeastern Europe, with a long coastline along the Adriatic Sea. It is known for its stunning beaches, picturesque islands, and ancient cities. If you're planning a trip to Croatia, it's important to know how to get around the country so you can fully experience all that it has to offer.

There are several options for getting around Croatia, including by car, bus, train, or plane.

Renting a car is a convenient option for getting around Croatia, as it allows you to travel at your own pace and explore the country's many small towns and villages. The roads in Croatia are generally in good condition, although some of the smaller roads may be winding and narrow. It's important to drive defensively, as some drivers in Croatia can be aggressive.

If you're planning to rent a car in Croatia, you will need to have a valid driver's license and an International Driving Permit (IDP). You can obtain an IDP from your local automobile association before your trip. It's also a good idea to purchase car insurance, as medical and repair costs can be expensive in Croatia.

The bus is another popular option for getting around Croatia. The country has a well-developed bus network, with buses running between most major cities and towns. The buses are generally comfortable and reliable, and tickets can be purchased at the bus station or online.

Croatia has a limited rail network, with trains running between major cities such as Zagreb, Split, and Rijeka. The trains are generally comfortable and offer a scenic way to travel, but they can be slower than other forms of transportation. Tickets can be purchased at the train station or online.

If you're planning to travel between Croatia's larger cities or islands, flying may be the most convenient option. Croatia has several airports, including Zagreb Airport, Split Airport, and Dubrovnik

Airport. Several airlines operate flights within Croatia, including Croatia Airlines and Ryanair.

Regardless of how you choose to get around Croatia, it's a good idea to plan you're itinerary and book your transportation and accommodations ahead of time. This will help ensure that you have a smooth and enjoyable trip.

Domestic Flights

Croatia has several airports that offer domestic flights within the country. The main airports are Zagreb Airport, Split Airport, and Dubrovnik Airport. There are several airlines that operate domestic flights within Croatia, including Croatia Airlines and Ryanair.

Croatia Airlines is the national carrier of Croatia and offers flights between major cities such as Zagreb, Split, and Dubrovnik. The airline operates a fleet of modern aircraft and offers a range of services, including in-flight entertainment and meals.

Ryanair is a low-cost airline that operates flights between several Croatian cities, including Zagreb, Split, and Dubrovnik. The airline offers competitive fares and operates a fleet of modern aircraft.

The price of domestic flights in Croatia can vary depending on the route, time of year, and demand. Generally, prices are higher during peak tourist season and on popular routes. It's a good idea to book your flights in advance to get the best price and availability.

To book a domestic flight in Croatia, you can visit the website of the airline or use an online travel agent. It's a good idea to compare prices and read reviews before booking to ensure you get the best deal.

In summary, several airports and airlines offer domestic flights within Croatia. Croatia Airlines is the national carrier and offers flights between major cities, while Ryanair is a low-cost airline that operates flights between several Croatian cities. The price of domestic flights in Croatia can vary depending on the route, time of year, and demand. It's a good idea to book your flights in advance to get the best price and availability.

Trains And Subways

Croatia has a limited rail network, with trains running between major cities such as Zagreb, Split, and Rijeka. The trains are generally comfortable and offer a scenic way to travel, although they can be slower than other forms of transportation.

There are two main types of trains in Croatia:

1. **InterCity (IC) trains:** These are the fastest and most comfortable trains in Croatia, with air conditioning and seating arrangements. They operate on major routes between cities and towns.

2. **Local trains:** These trains are slower and less comfortable than InterCity trains, with no air conditioning and less frequent service. They operate on smaller routes between towns and villages.

To ride the train in Croatia, you will need to purchase a ticket before boarding. Tickets can be purchased at the train station or online. It's a good idea to book your tickets in advance, especially during peak tourist season, as trains can be crowded.

There are no subways in Croatia. However, the city of Zagreb has a tram system that serves as the main form of public transportation within the city. The trams are efficient and convenient, with routes running throughout the city. To ride the tram in Zagreb, you will need to purchase a ticket before boarding. Tickets can be purchased at kiosks or from the driver.

Croatia has a limited rail network, with trains running between major cities such as Zagreb, Split, and Rijeka. There are two main types of trains in Croatia: InterCity trains, which are the fastest and most comfortable, and local trains, which are slower and less comfortable. To ride the train in Croatia, you will need to purchase a ticket before boarding, which can be done at the train station or online. There are no subways in Croatia, but the city of Zagreb has a tram system that serves as the main form of public transportation within the city. To ride the tram in Zagreb, you will need to purchase a ticket before boarding.

Buses And Long-Distance Coaches

The bus is a popular and convenient option for getting around Croatia, with a well-developed network that connects most major cities and towns. Buses in Croatia are generally comfortable and reliable, with air conditioning and modern amenities.

There are two main types of buses in Croatia:

1) **Local buses:** These buses operate within cities and towns and are a convenient option for shorter trips. They can be crowded during peak times and may not be as comfortable as long-distance coaches.

2) **Long-distance coaches:** These buses operate between cities and towns and are a comfortable and convenient option for longer trips. They offer more amenities than local buses, such as on-board toilets and refreshments.

To ride the bus in Croatia, you will need to purchase a ticket before boarding. Tickets can be purchased at the bus station or online. It's a good idea to book your tickets in advance, especially during peak tourist season, as buses can be crowded.

The bus is a popular and convenient option for getting around Croatia, with a well-developed network that connects most major cities and towns. There are two main types of buses in Croatia: local buses, which operate within cities and towns, and long-distance coaches, which operate between cities and towns and offer more amenities. To ride the bus in Croatia, you will need to purchase a ticket before boarding, which can be done at the bus station or online. It's a good idea to book your tickets in advance to ensure availability.

Rental Cars And Driving In Croatia

Renting a car is a convenient option for getting around Croatia, as it allows you to travel at your own pace and explore the country's many small towns and villages. The roads in Croatia are generally in good condition, although some of the smaller roads may be winding and narrow. It's important to drive defensively, as some drivers in Croatia can be aggressive.

If you're planning to rent a car in Croatia, you will need to have a valid driver's license and an International Driving Permit (IDP). You can obtain an IDP from your local automobile association before your trip. It's also a good idea to purchase car insurance, as medical and repair costs can be expensive in Croatia.

Several rental car companies operate in Croatia, including international brands such as Avis, Hertz, and Europcar, as well as local companies. You can book a rental car online or at the rental car office at the airport or in the city. It's a good idea to compare prices and read reviews before booking to ensure you get the best deal.

When driving in Croatia, it's important to follow the local traffic laws and regulations. In Croatia, you must drive on the right side of the road and pass on the left. The speed limit is generally 50 km/h in urban areas and 80 km/h on highways. It's also important to wear your seatbelt at all times and to use your headlights when driving at night or in poor visibility.

To rent a car in Croatia, you will need to follow these steps:

Determine your travel dates and location. Consider the availability of rental cars in the area you will be visiting and the duration of your trip to find the best options.

Search for rental car companies. Several rental car companies operate in Croatia, including international brands such as Avis, Hertz, and Europcar, as well as local companies. You can search for rental car companies online or at the airport or in the city.

Compare prices and read reviews. It's a good idea to compare prices and read reviews from other customers before booking to ensure you get the best deal.

Book your rental car. Once you have found a rental car that meets your needs, you can book it online or at the rental car office. You will need to provide your personal and payment information to complete the booking process.

Pick up your rental car. When you arrive at the rental car office, you will need to present your driver's license and International Driving Permit (IDP) to pick up your rental car. You will also need to sign a rental agreement and pay any applicable fees.

Renting a car is a convenient option for getting around Croatia and allows you to explore the country at your own pace. You will need to have a valid driver's license and an International Driving Permit to rent a car in Croatia, and it's a good idea to purchase car insurance. Several rental car companies operate in Croatia, and you can book a rental car online or at the rental car office. When driving in Croatia, it's important to follow the local traffic laws and regulations, including driving on the right side of the road and using your headlights when driving at night or in poor visibility.

CHAPTER 4: ACCOMMODATION IN CROATIA

Croatia is a beautiful country located in southeastern Europe, known for its stunning Adriatic coast, ancient castles, and charming villages. It's no surprise that it has become a popular destination for travelers from all over the world.

When it comes to finding accommodation in Croatia, there are a variety of options available. From luxurious hotels and resorts to more budget-friendly options like hostels and apartments, there is something for every traveler's needs and preferences.

One of the most popular types of accommodation in Croatia is the traditional Croatian stone house, or "kamenica," which can be found in many of the country's rural villages. These houses are typically made of stone and offer a rustic, authentic experience for travelers.

For those looking for something a bit more modern, there are plenty of hotels and resorts located along the Adriatic coast, offering breathtaking views of the sea and access to a variety of amenities. There are also many apartments and holiday homes available for rent, which can be a great option for families or groups traveling together.

No matter what type of accommodation you choose, you can be sure that you will be welcomed with warm Croatian hospitality and have an unforgettable stay in this beautiful country.

Hotels

Luxury hotels:

Croatia is a beautiful Mediterranean country known for its stunning coastline, rich history and culture, and vibrant cities. If you're looking for a luxurious vacation experience, there are many luxury hotels in Croatia to choose from.

Hotel Excelsior Dubrovnik: The Hotel Excelsior Dubrovnik is a luxurious five-star hotel located in the heart of Dubrovnik, a historic city on the Adriatic coast of Croatia. The hotel is situated on a beautiful stretch of coastline, offering breathtaking views of the city and the sea.

The Hotel Excelsior Dubrovnik is known for its opulent and sophisticated design, with elegant guest rooms and suites that are decorated in a classic, refined style. The hotel offers a range of room types, including standard rooms, deluxe rooms, and executive suites, all of which are equipped with modern amenities such as flat-screen TVs and Wi-Fi. Some rooms offer private balconies or terraces with stunning views of the city and the sea.

The Hotel Excelsior Dubrovnik offers a range of luxurious amenities for guests to enjoy, including fine dining at the hotel's two restaurants, the Atlantic and the Excelsior. The hotel also has a spa and a fitness center, as well as a private beach and a rooftop pool with panoramic views of the city and the sea.

To book a stay at the Hotel Excelsior Dubrovnik, you can visit the hotel's website or contact the hotel directly to make a reservation. You can also book a stay at the Hotel Excelsior Dubrovnik through a travel booking website or a travel agent. When booking a stay at the hotel, be sure to check the availability and rates for the dates you are interested in, as well as any special offers or packages that may be available

Rixos Premium Dubrovnik: Rixos Premium Dubrovnik is a luxurious five-star hotel located in Dubrovnik, a historic city on the Adriatic coast of Croatia. The hotel is situated on a beautiful stretch of coastline, offering breathtaking views of the city and the sea.

The Rixos Premium Dubrovnik is known for its elegant and modern design, with guest rooms and suites that are stylishly furnished and equipped with a range of amenities such as flat-screen TVs, Wi-Fi, and minibars. Some rooms offer private balconies or terraces with stunning views of the city and the sea.

The Rixos Premium Dubrovnik offers a range of luxurious amenities for guests to enjoy, including fine dining at the hotel's several restaurants, a spa and fitness center, and a private beach. The hotel also has a rooftop pool with panoramic views of the city and the sea.

In addition to its luxurious amenities, the Rixos Premium Dubrovnik is also known for its excellent location. The hotel is situated within walking distance of Dubrovnik's Old Town, a UNESCO World Heritage site that is home to several historic landmarks and attractions. The hotel is also located near several popular beaches, making it an ideal choice for travelers who want to relax on the beach or explore the beautiful Adriatic coastline.

To book a stay at the Rixos Premium Dubrovnik, you can visit the hotel's website or contact the hotel directly to make a reservation. You can also book a stay at the Rixos Premium Dubrovnik through a travel booking website or a travel agent. When booking a stay at the hotel, be sure to check the availability and rates for the dates you are interested in, as well as any special offers or packages that may be available.

Hilton Imperial Dubrovnik: The Hilton Imperial Dubrovnik is a luxurious five-star hotel located in Dubrovnik, a historic city on the Adriatic coast of Croatia. The hotel is situated in the heart of the city, offering easy access to a range of attractions and amenities.

The Hilton Imperial Dubrovnik is known for its elegant and sophisticated design, with guest rooms and suites that are stylishly furnished and equipped with a range of amenities such as flat-screen TVs, Wi-Fi, and minibars. Some rooms offer private balconies or terraces with stunning views of the city and the sea.

The Hilton Imperial Dubrovnik offers a range of luxurious amenities for guests to enjoy, including fine dining at the hotel's restaurants, a spa and fitness center, and a private beach. The hotel also has an outdoor pool with panoramic views of the city and the sea.

In addition to its luxurious amenities, the Hilton Imperial Dubrovnik is also known for its excellent location. The hotel is situated within walking distance of Dubrovnik's Old Town, a UNESCO World Heritage site that is home to several historic landmarks and attractions. The hotel is also located near several popular beaches, making it an ideal choice for travelers who want to relax on the beach or explore the beautiful Adriatic coastline.

To book a stay at the Hilton Imperial Dubrovnik, you can visit the hotel's website or contact the hotel directly to make a reservation. You can also book a stay at the Hilton Imperial Dubrovnik through a travel booking website or a travel agent. When booking a stay at the hotel, be sure to check the availability and rates for the dates you are interested in, as well as any special offers or packages that may be available.

Hotel Esplanade Zagreb: The Hotel Esplanade Zagreb is a luxurious five-star hotel located in the heart of Zagreb, the capital city of Croatia. The hotel is known for its grand and opulent Art Deco design and is a popular choice for travelers looking for a luxurious and sophisticated stay in the city.

The Hotel Esplanade Zagreb offers a range of guest rooms and suites that are stylishly furnished and equipped with a range of amenities such as flat-screen TVs, Wi-Fi, and minibars. Some rooms offer private balconies or terraces with stunning views of the city.

The Hotel Esplanade Zagreb offers a range of luxurious amenities for guests to enjoy, including fine dining at the hotel's restaurants, a spa and fitness center, and a rooftop pool with panoramic views of the city. The hotel also has several meeting and event spaces, making it an ideal choice for business travelers or for hosting special events.

In addition to its luxurious amenities, the Hotel Esplanade Zagreb is also known for its excellent location. The hotel is situated in the heart of Zagreb, within walking distance of a range of attractions and amenities. The hotel is also located near the main train station, making it an easy choice for travelers arriving by train.

To book a stay at the Hotel Esplanade Zagreb, you can visit the hotel's website or contact the hotel directly to make a reservation. You can also book a stay at the Hotel Esplanade Zagreb through a travel booking website or a travel agent. When booking a stay at the hotel, be sure to check the availability and rates for the dates you are interested in, as well as any special offers or packages that may be available.

Hotel Ariston, Split: The Hotel Ariston is a chic and modern luxury hotel located in the heart of Split, a vibrant city on the Adriatic coast of Croatia. The hotel is known for its sleek and contemporary design and is a popular choice for travelers looking for a luxurious and stylish stay in the city.

The Hotel Ariston offers a range of guest rooms and suites that are stylishly furnished and equipped with a range of amenities such as flat-screen TVs, Wi-Fi, and minibars. Some rooms offer private balconies or terraces with stunning views of the city.

The Hotel Ariston offers a range of luxurious amenities for guests to enjoy, including fine dining at the hotel's restaurant, a spa and fitness center, and a rooftop pool with panoramic views of the city. The hotel also has several meeting and event spaces, making it an ideal choice for business travelers or for hosting special events.

In addition to its luxurious amenities, the Hotel Ariston is also known for its excellent location. The hotel is situated in the heart of Split, within walking distance of a range of attractions and amenities. The hotel is also located near the main train station, making it an easy choice for travelers arriving by train.

To book a stay at the Hotel Ariston, you can visit the hotel's website or contact the hotel directly to make a reservation. You can also book a stay at the Hotel

Ariston through a travel booking website or a travel agent. When booking a stay at the hotel, be sure to check the availability and rates for the dates you are interested in, as well as any special offers or packages that

Hotel Lone, Rovinj: The Hotel Lone is a luxury five-star hotel located in Rovinj, a charming coastal town on the Adriatic coast of Croatia. The hotel is known for its modern and sleek design and is a popular choice for travelers looking for a luxurious and stylish stay in the region.

The Hotel Lone offers a range of guest rooms and suites that are stylishly furnished and equipped with a range of amenities such as flat-screen TVs, Wi-Fi, and minibars. Some rooms offer private balconies or terraces with stunning views of the town and the sea.

The Hotel Lone offers a range of luxurious amenities for guests to enjoy, including fine dining at the hotel's restaurant, a spa and fitness center, and a rooftop pool with panoramic views of the town and the sea. The hotel also has several meeting and event spaces, making it an ideal choice for business travelers or for hosting special events.

In addition to its luxurious amenities, the Hotel Lone is also known for its excellent location. The hotel is situated in the heart of Rovinj, within walking distance of a range of attractions and amenities. The hotel is also located near the town's main beach, making it an easy choice for travelers looking to relax on the beach or explore the beautiful Adriatic coastline.

To book a stay at the Hotel Lone, you can visit the hotel's website or contact the hotel directly to make a reservation. You can also book a stay at the Hotel Lone through a travel booking website or a travel agent. When booking a stay at the hotel, be sure to check the availability and rates for the dates you are interested in, as well as any special offers or packages that may be available.

Hotel Park, Mlini: The Hotel Park is a luxury four-star hotel located in Mlini, a charming coastal town on the Adriatic coast of Croatia. The hotel is known for its modern and stylish design and is a popular choice for travelers looking for a luxurious and comfortable stay in the region.

The Hotel Park offers a range of guest rooms and suites that are stylishly furnished and equipped with a range of amenities such as flat-screen TVs, Wi-Fi, and minibars. Some rooms offer private balconies or terraces with stunning views of the town and the sea. The Hotel Park offers a range of luxurious amenities for guests to enjoy, including fine dining at the hotel's restaurant, a spa and fitness center, and an outdoor pool with panoramic views of the town and the sea. The hotel also has several meeting and event spaces, making it an ideal choice for business travelers or for hosting special events.

In addition to its luxurious amenities, the Hotel Park is also known for its excellent location. The hotel is situated in the heart of Mlini, within walking distance of a range of attractions and amenities. The hotel is also located near the town's main beach, making it an easy choice for travelers looking to relax on the beach or explore the beautiful Adriatic coastline.

To book a stay at the Hotel Park, you can visit the hotel's website or contact the hotel directly to make a reservation. You can also book a stay at the Hotel Park through a travel booking website or a travel agent. When booking a stay at the hotel, be sure to check the availability and rates for the dates you are interested in, as well as any special offers or packages that may be available.

Mid-range hotels:

Mid-range hotels in Croatia offer travelers a comfortable and affordable option for accommodation while exploring this beautiful country. With a variety of amenities and room types available, these hotels are a popular choice for travelers of all types, from families to solo travelers to couples.

When booking a mid-range hotel in Croatia, it's important to consider the location of the hotel and the amenities it offers. Many mid-range hotels are located in popular tourist destinations such as

Dubrovnik, Split, and Zagreb, and offer a range of room types to suit different needs, including standard rooms, superior rooms, and family rooms. In terms of amenities, most mid-range hotels in Croatia offer a swimming pool, fitness center, and restaurant. Some also offer additional facilities such as a spa or wellness center, making them an ideal choice for travelers looking to relax and rejuvenate during their vacation.

There are several ways to book a mid-range hotel in Croatia. One option is to search online travel websites such as Expedia, Booking.com, or Hotels.com, which offer a wide range of hotels at different price points. These websites allow you to search for hotels based on location, price, and amenities, making it easy to find the perfect hotel for your needs.

Another option is to contact a local travel agency, which can help you find a hotel that meets your specific requirements. These agencies often have access to special rates and packages that may not be available through online booking websites, so it's worth considering if you are looking for the best deal.

Once you have found a hotel that meets your needs, you can typically book it directly through the hotel's website or an online booking website. It's a good idea to read reviews from previous guests and to compare prices from different sources to ensure you are getting the best deal.

It's also worth considering the location of the hotel when booking. Many mid-range hotels in Croatia are located in popular tourist destinations, such as Dubrovnik, Split, and Zagreb, which offer a range of activities and attractions for travelers. These cities are well-connected by public transportation, making it easy to explore the surrounding area.

If you are planning to visit more rural or less touristy areas of Croatia, it may be worth considering a mid-range hotel in a smaller town or village. These hotels often offer a more authentic and local experience and may be less crowded and more peaceful than hotels in larger cities.

When booking a mid-range hotel in Croatia, it's important to read the terms and conditions carefully, as these can vary between hotels and booking websites. Some hotels may require a deposit to be paid at the time of booking and may have cancellation policies that vary depending on the length of your stay.

Mid-range hotels in Croatia offer a range of amenities and room types at an affordable price, and there are several options for booking to suit different needs and budgets. Whether you are planning a family vacation, a romantic getaway, or a solo trip, you can find a mid-range hotel in Croatia to suit your needs.

Budget-Friendly Options:

Budget-friendly options in Croatia offer travelers a cost-effective way to explore this beautiful country without breaking the bank. Whether you are a student, a backpacker, or simply looking for an affordable vacation, there are many budget-friendly options in Croatia to suit different needs and preferences.

One budget-friendly option for accommodation in Croatia is hostels. Hostels are a popular choice for budget travelers, as they offer shared dormitory-style rooms at a lower cost than hotels. Many hostels in Croatia also offer private rooms for a slightly higher price, making them a good option for travelers who prefer a bit more privacy.

Hostels in Croatia typically offer a range of amenities such as shared kitchen facilities, a common area, and free Wi-Fi. Some also offer additional facilities such as a swimming pool or a bar, making them a fun and social option for travellers.

Another budget-friendly option in Croatia is camping. Croatia has several campsites located throughout the country, many of which offer basic amenities such as showers, toilets, and electricity. Some campsites also offer more luxurious options such as glamping tents or rental mobile homes.

Camping is a great option for travelers who are looking for an affordable and authentic way to experience Croatia. It's also a good option for those who are traveling by their transportation, as many campsites are located in more rural areas and may not be easily accessible by public transport.

To book a budget-friendly option in Croatia, you can search online booking websites such as Hostelworld or Booking.com, which offer a range of hostels and campsites at different price points. You can also contact a local travel agency, which may have access to special rates and packages.

It's a good idea to read reviews from previous guests and to compare prices from different sources to ensure you are getting the best deal. It's also worth considering the location of the hostel or campsite, as this can affect the cost and the convenience of your stay.

Vacation Rentals

vacation rentals, such as apartments or holiday homes. These rentals offer travelers the opportunity to have their own private space and kitchen facilities, which can be a more economical option than staying in a hotel, especially for longer stays or for travelers in a group.

Vacation rentals in Croatia can be found through online booking websites such as Airbnb or VRBO, or local rental agencies. It's a good idea to compare prices and read reviews from previous guests to ensure you are getting the best deal.

Private Rentals (e.g. Apartments, Houses):

Private rentals, such as apartments and holiday homes, are a popular option for travelers looking for more independent and private accommodation in Croatia. These rentals offer travelers the opportunity to have their own private space and kitchen facilities, which can be a more economical option than staying in a hotel, especially for longer stays or for travelers in a group.

Private rentals in Croatia can be found through online booking websites such as Airbnb or VRBO, or local rental agencies. It's a good idea to compare prices and read reviews from previous guests to ensure you are getting the best deal.

When booking a private rental in Croatia, it's important to consider the location and the amenities that are included. Some rentals may be located in more rural areas, while others may be located in popular tourist destinations. It's also worth considering the type of rental that is best suited to your needs, such as a studio apartment for solo travelers or a larger vacation home for a group.

In terms of location, Croatia has a range of destinations to choose from, including the historic cities of Dubrovnik and Split, the stunning beaches of the Dalmatian Coast, and the picturesque islands of the Adriatic Sea. No matter what type of vacation you are planning, you can find a private rental in Croatia to suit your needs.

In terms of amenities, private rentals in Croatia can vary widely. Some rentals may include basic facilities such as a kitchen and a bathroom, while others may offer additional amenities such as a swimming pool, a barbecue, or a terrace. It's a good idea to consider what amenities are important to you when choosing a rental.

To book a private rental in Croatia, you can search online booking websites such as Airbnb or VRBO, or contact a local rental agency. It's a good idea to read the terms and conditions carefully, as these can vary between rentals and booking websites. Some rentals may require a deposit to be paid at the time of booking and may have cancellation policies that vary depending on the length of your stay.

One advantage of private rentals in Croatia is the flexibility they offer. Many rentals are available for short or long-term stays, allowing travelers to tailor their vacation to their specific needs and preferences. For example, if you are planning a longer stay in Croatia, a private rental can be a more economical option than a hotel, as you can save money by cooking your meals and having your own space.

Private rentals in Croatia can also be a good option for travelers who are looking for a more authentic and local experience. By staying in a rental in a residential neighborhood, you can get a sense of what it's like to live in Croatia and interact with the local community. Many rentals also offer the opportunity to meet and connect with the owner or property manager, who can provide insights and recommendations on the area.

When booking a private rental in Croatia, it's important to communicate with the owner or property manager to ensure that the rental meets your specific needs and expectations. This may include asking about the location, the amenities, and the availability of parking or public transportation.

It's also a good idea to read the reviews from previous guests, as these can provide valuable insights into the rental and the owner. If you have any special requests or concerns, it's important to raise them with the owner or property manager before booking.

Private rentals in Croatia, such as apartments and holiday homes, offer travelers a more independent and private accommodation option while exploring this beautiful country. With a range of locations and amenities available, and several options for booking, travelers can find the perfect rental to suit their needs and budget.

Rental Agencies And Booking Websites:

Rental agencies and booking websites are a convenient and efficient way to book accommodation in Croatia. These services offer a wide range of options, including hotels, vacation rentals, hostels, and campsites, at different price points, making it easy to find the perfect accommodation to suit your needs and budget.

Rental agencies are local companies that specialize in renting out properties, such as apartments, holiday homes, and villas, in a specific region or destination. These agencies typically have a portfolio of properties that they manage and can help travelers find the right rental to suit their needs. Rental agencies often offer additional services such as property management, maintenance, and cleaning, making them a convenient choice for travelers.

Booking websites are online platforms that allow travelers to search for and book accommodation in Croatia and around the world. These websites typically offer a wide range of options, including hotels, vacation rentals, hostels, and campsites, at different price points. Booking websites also offer a range of filters and search tools to help travelers find the perfect accommodation to suit their needs, such as location, price, and amenities.

To book accommodation through a rental agency or booking website, travelers can search the website for options in their desired destination and dates. They can then compare prices and read reviews from previous guests to find the best deal. Once they have found the right accommodation, they can typically book it directly through the website and pay with a credit card or other payment method.

It's a good idea to read the terms and conditions carefully when booking through a rental agency or booking website, as these can vary between providers. Some agencies or websites may require a deposit to be paid at the time of booking and may have cancellation policies that vary depending on the length of your stay.

advantage of booking through a rental agency or booking website is the convenience it offers. These services allow travelers to compare prices and options from different providers in one place, saving time and effort. They also offer secure online payment options, making it easy and safe to pay for your accommodation.

Another advantage is the range of options available. Rental agencies and booking websites offer a wide range of accommodation types, from hotels and vacation rentals to hostels and campsites, making it easy to find the right option to suit your needs and budget. These services also offer a range of filters and search tools, such as location, price, and amenities, to help travelers find the perfect accommodation.

One potential disadvantage of booking through a rental agency or booking website is that you may not have as much control over your accommodation as you would if you were booking directly with the property owner or manager. For example, you may not be able to negotiate special rates or request specific amenities. It's a good idea to read the terms and conditions carefully and to communicate with the property owner or manager to ensure that your accommodation meets your expectations.

Rental agencies and booking websites are a convenient and efficient way to book accommodation in Croatia. These services offer a wide range of options at different price points and provide travelers with the tools and information they need to find the perfect accommodation to suit their needs.

Hostels And Guesthouses

Hostels and guesthouses are popular accommodation choices for travelers in Croatia, offering a more budget-friendly and social alternative to traditional hotels.

Hostels in Croatia are typically dormitory-style accommodations that offer shared rooms with bunk beds and shared bathrooms. They often have a common area where travelers can socialize and meet other travelers, as well as a kitchen where guests can prepare their meals. Hostels are a great option for solo travelers or small groups looking to save money on accommodation while still having access to amenities such as Wi-Fi and laundry facilities.

Guesthouses in Croatia are similar to hostels but typically offer private rooms with en-suite bathrooms. They may also have shared common areas and kitchens, and often have a more homely atmosphere than larger hotels. Guesthouses are a good choice for travelers who want a bit more privacy and comfort, but still want to stay in budget-friendly accommodations.

There are many websites where you can book hostels and guesthouses in Croatia. Some popular options include:

Hostelworld: This website offers a wide range of hostels and guesthouses in Croatia, as well as other budget accommodation options such as bed and breakfasts and apartments. It has a user-friendly booking platform and allows you to filter your search by location, price, and ratings.

Booking.com: This website offers a wide range of accommodation options in Croatia, including hostels and guesthouses. It has a user-friendly booking platform and allows you to filter your search by location, price, and ratings.

Airbnb: This website allows you to book private rooms or entire apartments in Croatia. It has a large selection of budget-friendly accommodation options, including hostels and guesthouses.

When booking a hostel or guesthouse in Croatia, it's important to carefully read the reviews and ratings from previous guests to get an idea of the quality of the accommodation and the level of service you can expect. It's also a good idea to check the cancellation policy before booking, as some hostels and guesthouses may have stricter policies than others.

CHAPTER 5: THINGS TO DO IN CROATIA

Sightseeing And Cultural Attractions

Croatia is a beautiful country located in Southeast Europe, known for its stunning Adriatic Sea coast, picturesque islands, and rich cultural heritage. From ancient Roman ruins to medieval castles and fortresses, there are plenty of sightseeing and cultural attractions to explore in Croatia. Here are some of the top ones:

- **Dubrovnik:** Dubrovnik is a UNESCO World Heritage site and a popular destination for tourists. It is known for its medieval walled city, which features winding streets, charming squares, and historical landmarks such as the Rector's Palace, Sponza Palace, and St. Blaise's Church. Visitors can also take a walk along the city walls for panoramic views of the city and the Adriatic Sea.

- **Plitvice Lakes National Park:** Located in central Croatia, Plitvice Lakes National Park is a stunning natural wonder, known for its series of interconnected lakes, waterfalls, and forests. The park is home to a wide variety of flora and fauna, and visitors can enjoy hiking, fishing, and boating. There are also several educational trails and guided tours available.

- Split: Split is the second-largest city in Croatia and is located on the Adriatic coast. It is known for its beautiful beaches, ancient Roman ruins, and the Diocletian's Palace, a UNESCO World Heritage site. The palace is an ancient Roman palace that was later transformed into a fortress. It is home to several historical landmarks, including the Cathedral of St. Domnius, the Temple of Jupiter, and the Peristyle.

- **Zagreb:** Zagreb is the capital and largest city of Croatia, known for its rich cultural heritage and stunning architecture. The city is home to several museums, galleries, and theaters, including the Museum of Broken Relationships, the Croatian Museum of Naive Art, and the

Croatian National Theater. Visitors can also explore the city's Old Town, which is home to the Zagreb Cathedral, St. Mark's Church, and the Upper Town.

- **Hvar:** Hvar is a Croatian island located in the Adriatic Sea, known for its stunning beaches, crystal clear waters, and charming towns. The island is home to several cultural attractions, including the Hvar Fortress, St. Stephen's Cathedral, and the Hvar Heritage Museum. Visitors can also enjoy hiking, biking, and water sports on the island.
- Rovinj: Rovinj is a charming coastal town located on the western coast of the Istrian Peninsula. It is known for its narrow streets,

colorful houses, and beautiful beaches. Visitors can explore the Old Town, which is home to the Church of St. Euphemia, the Rovinj Heritage Museum, and the Rovinj Art Gallery. The town is also surrounded by beautiful natural parks, including the Lim Channel and the Golden Cape Forest Park.

- **Pula:** Pula is a city located on the Istrian Peninsula, known for its rich history and cultural heritage. It is home to several ancient Roman landmarks, including the Pula Arena, the Temple of Augustus, and the Arch of the Sergii. Visitors can also explore the Pula Archaeological Museum, which houses a collection of artifacts from the Roman and ancient Greek periods.

- **Korčula:** Korčula is an island located in the Adriatic Sea, known for its charming Old Town, beautiful beaches, and rich cultural heritage. The island is home to several historical landmarks, including the Cathedral of St. Mark, the St. Michael's Fortress, and the Museum of Icons. Visitors can also enjoy a variety of outdoor activities on the island, such as hiking, cycling, and water sports.

- **Trogir:** Trogir is a small town located on the Adriatic coast, known for its medieval Old Town, which is a UNESCO World Heritage site. The town is home to several historical landmarks, including the Cathedral of St. Lawrence, the St.

John's Fortress, and the Radovan's Portal. Visitors can also explore the Town Museum, which houses a collection of artifacts from the ancient Roman, medieval, and modern periods.

- **Šibenik:** Šibenik is a city located on the Dalmatian coast, known for its rich cultural heritage and stunning natural beauty. The city is home to several historical landmarks, including the Cathedral of St. James, the Fortress of St. Michael, and the Šibenik City Museum. Visitors can also explore the city's beautiful beaches and nearby islands, such as the Kornati National Park.

Temples and shrines:

Croatia is a country with a rich cultural heritage and a long history of religious traditions. As such, there are several temples and shrines scattered throughout the country that are worth visiting for their architectural, historical, and cultural significance. Here are some of the top temples and shrines in Croatia:

- **The Cathedral of St. James in Šibenik:** Located in the city of Šibenik, the Cathedral of St. James is a UNESCO World Heritage site and one of the most important cultural landmarks in Croatia. It is a Roman Catholic cathedral that was built in the 15th and 16th centuries and is known for its Gothic and Renaissance architecture. The cathedral is home to several valuable artworks, including a stunning altarpiece by the Croatian artist Juraj Dalmatinac.

- **The Church of the Holy Spirit in Dubrovnik:** The Church of the Holy Spirit is a Roman Catholic church located in the city of Dubrovnik. It is known for its Gothic architecture and beautiful frescoes, which depict scenes from the life of Jesus and the Virgin Mary. The church is also home to several valuable artworks, including a goldsmith's workshop and a collection of religious artifacts.

- **The Cathedral of St. Domnius in Split:** Located in the city of Split, the Cathedral of St.

Domnius is a Roman Catholic cathedral that was built in the 4th century. It is known for its stunning architecture and rich history and is home to several valuable artworks, including a beautiful altarpiece by the Croatian artist Andrija Aleši.

- **The Church of St. Mary in Zadar:** The Church of St. Mary is a Roman Catholic church located in the city of Zadar. It is known for its beautiful Gothic architecture and stunning frescoes, which depict scenes from the life of Jesus and the Virgin Mary. The church is also home to several valuable artworks, including a collection of religious artifacts and a goldsmith's workshop.

- **The Church of St. Nicholas in Zagreb:** Located in the city of Zagreb, the Church of St. Nicholas is a Roman Catholic church that was built in the 13th century. It is known for its beautiful Gothic architecture and stunning frescoes, which depict scenes from the life of Jesus and the Virgin Mary. The church is also home to several valuable artworks, including a collection of religious artifacts and a goldsmith's workshop.

- **The Church of St. Mary in Hvar:** Located on the island of Hvar, the Church of St. Mary is a Roman Catholic church that was built in the 16th century. It is known for its beautiful Renaissance architecture and stunning frescoes, which depict scenes from the life of Jesus and the Virgin Mary. The church is also home to several valuable artworks, including a collection of religious artifacts and a goldsmith's workshop.

- **The Church of St. Lawrence in Rovinj:** Located in the town of Rovinj, the Church of St. Lawrence is a Roman Catholic church that was built in the 18th century. It is known for its beautiful Baroque architecture and stunning frescoes, which depict scenes from the life of Jesus and the Virgin Mary. The church is also home to several valuable artworks, including a collection of religious artifacts and a goldsmith's workshop.

- **The Church of the Assumption in Korčula:** Located on the island of Korčula, the Church of the Assumption is a Roman Catholic church that was built in the 14th century. It is known for its beautiful Gothic architecture and stunning frescoes, which depict scenes from the life of Jesus and the Virgin Mary. The church is also home to several valuable artworks, including a collection of religious artifacts and a goldsmith's workshop.

- **The Church of St. Mary in Pula:** Located in the city of Pula, the Church of St. Mary is a Roman Catholic church that was built in the 14th century. It is known for its beautiful Gothic architecture and stunning frescoes, which depict scenes from the life of Jesus and the Virgin Mary. The church is also home to several valuable artworks, including a collection of religious artifacts and a goldsmith's workshop.

- **The Church of St. John in Trogir:** Located in the town of Trogir, the Church of St. John is a Roman Catholic church that was built in the 13th century. It is known for its beautiful Gothic architecture and stunning frescoes, which depict scenes from the life of Jesus and the Virgin Mary. The church is also home to several valuable artworks, including a collection of religious artifacts and a goldsmith's workshop.

Museums And Galleries:

Here are some of the top museums and galleries in Croatia:

- **The Croatian Museum of Naive Art in Zagreb:** Located in the capital city of Zagreb, the Croatian Museum of Naive Art is dedicated to the art of Croatian naive artists. The museum houses a collection of paintings, sculptures, and other works by some of the most notable Croatian naive artists, including Ivan Generalić, Mirko Lovrak, and Ivan Rabuzin.

- **The Museum of Broken Relationships in Zagreb:** Located in the capital city of Zagreb, the Museum of Broken Relationships is a unique museum that is dedicated to the theme of love and relationships. The museum houses a collection of objects and artifacts that were donated by people from around the world, and each object is accompanied by a story about a past relationship.

- **The Croatian National Theater in Zagreb:** Located in the capital city of Zagreb, the Croatian National Theater is a performing arts venue that is home to the Croatian National Theater in Zagreb opera, ballet, and drama companies. The theater is known for its stunning architecture and beautiful interior, and it hosts a variety of performances throughout the year.

- **The Pula Archaeological Museum:** Located in the city of Pula, the Pula Archaeological Museum is dedicated to the history and culture of the region. The museum houses a collection of artifacts from the ancient Roman, medieval, and modern periods, including a collection of ancient Roman coins and a replica of a Roman gladiator's armor.

- **The Dubrovnik City Museum:** Located in the city of Dubrovnik, the Dubrovnik City Museum is dedicated to the history and culture of the region. The museum houses a collection of artifacts from the ancient Roman, medieval, and modern periods, including a collection of ancient

Roman coins and a replica of a Roman gladiator's armor.

- **The Rovinj Heritage Museum:** Located in the town of Rovinj, the Rovinj Heritage Museum is dedicated to the history and culture of the region. The museum houses a collection of artifacts from the ancient Roman, medieval, and modern periods, including a collection of ancient Roman coins and a replica of a Roman gladiator's armor.

- **The Zadar City Museum:** Located in the city of Zadar, the Zadar City Museum is dedicated to the history and culture of the region. The museum houses a collection of artifacts from the ancient Roman, medieval, and modern periods, including a collection of ancient Roman coins and a replica of a Roman gladiator's armor.

- **The Hvar Heritage Museum:** Located on the island of Hvar, the Hvar Heritage Museum is dedicated to the history and culture of the region. The museum houses a collection of artifacts from the ancient Roman, medieval, and modern periods, including a collection of ancient Roman coins and a replica of a Roman gladiator's armor.

- **The Šibenik City Museum:** Located in the city of Šibenik, the Šibenik City Museum is dedicated to the history and culture of the region. The museum houses a collection of artifacts from the ancient Roman, medieval, and modern periods, including a collection of ancient Roman coins and a replica of a Roman gladiator's armor.

- **The Split City Museum:** Located in the city of Split, the Split City Museum is dedicated to the history and culture of the region. The museum houses a collection of artifacts from the ancient Roman, medieval, and modern periods, including a collection of ancient Roman coins and a replica of a Roman gladiator's armor.

Landmarks And Historical Sites:

landmarks and historical sites scattered throughout the country that are worth visiting for their educational and cultural value. Here are some of the top landmarks and historical sites in Croatia:

- **The Rector's Palace in Dubrovnik:** Located in the city of Dubrovnik, the Rector's Palace is a Renaissance palace that was built in the 15th century. It is known for its stunning architecture and beautiful interior, and it houses several valuable artworks and artifacts, including a collection of ancient Roman coins and a replica of a Roman gladiator's armor.

- **The Diocletian's Palace in Split:** Located in the city of Split, the Diocletian's Palace is a UNESCO World Heritage site and one of the most important cultural landmarks in Croatia. It is an ancient Roman palace that was later transformed into a fortress. It is home to several historical landmarks, including the Cathedral of St. Domnius, the Temple of Jupiter, and the Peristyle.

- **The Pula Arena:** Located in the city of Pula, the Pula Arena is an ancient Roman amphitheater that was built in the 1st century AD. It is one of the best-preserved amphitheaters in the world and is known for its stunning architecture and beautiful interior. The arena is still used for concerts and other events today.

- **The St. Blaise's Church in Dubrovnik:** Located in the city of Dubrovnik, St. Blaise's Church is a Baroque-style church that was built in the 18th century. It is known for its stunning architecture and beautiful interior, and it houses several valuable artworks and artifacts, including a collection of ancient Roman coins and a replica of a Roman gladiator's armor.

- **The Zagreb Cathedral:** Located in the capital city of Zagreb, the Zagreb Cathedral is a Roman Catholic cathedral that was built in the 13th century. It is known for its stunning Gothic architecture and beautiful interior, and it houses several valuable artworks and artifacts, including a collection of ancient Roman coins and a replica of a Roman gladiator's armor.

- The Old Town of Rovinj: Located in the town of Rovinj, the Old Town is a charming area that is known for its narrow streets, colorful houses, and beautiful architecture. The Old Town is home to several historical landmarks, including the Church of St. Euphemia, the Rovinj Heritage Museum, and the Rovinj Art Gallery.

- **The St. Michael's Fortress in Šibenik:** Located in the city of Šibenik, the St. Michael's Fortress is a medieval fortress that was built in the 15th century. It is known for its stunning architecture and beautiful views of the surrounding area, and it is a popular destination for tourists.

- **The Cathedral of St. James in Šibenik:** Located in the city of Šibenik, the Cathedral of St. James is a UNESCO World Heritage site and one of the most important cultural landmarks in Croatia. It is a Roman Catholic cathedral that was built in the 15th and 16th centuries and is known for its Gothic and Renaissance architecture.

- **The St. John's Fortress in Trogir:** Located in the town of Trogir, the St. John's Fortress is a medieval fortress that was built in the 13th century. It is known for its stunning architecture and beautiful views of the surrounding area, and it is a popular destination for tourists.

- **The Radovan's Portal in Trogir:** Located in the town of Trogir, the Radovan's Portal is a Gothic-style portal that was built in the 13th century. It is known for its beautiful carvings and intricate details, and it is a popular destination for tourists.

Outdoor Activities And Nature

Hiking And Mountain Climbing:

Here are some of the top destinations for hiking and mountain climbing in Croatia:

- **The Plitvice Lakes National Park:** Located in central Croatia, the Plitvice Lakes National Park is a UNESCO World Heritage site and one of the most popular destinations for hiking and mountain climbing in the country. The park is home to a series of beautiful lakes and waterfalls, and several trails wind through the park, ranging in difficulty from easy to challenging.

- **The Velebit Mountain Range:** Located in central Croatia, the Velebit Mountain Range is a popular destination for hiking and mountain climbing. The range is home to several trails that offer breathtaking views of the surrounding landscape, and there are a variety of routes available, ranging in difficulty from easy to challenging.

- **The Risnjak National Park:** Located in northwest Croatia, the Risnjak National Park is a beautiful natural park that is home to a variety of hiking and mountain-climbing trails. The park is known for its stunning views of the surrounding landscape and its diverse plant and animal life.

- **The Biokovo Nature Park:** Located on the Dalmatian coast, the Biokovo Nature Park is a beautiful natural park that is home to a variety of hiking and mountain-climbing trails. The park is known for its stunning views of the surrounding landscape and its diverse plant and animal life.

- **The Medvednica Mountain:** Located near the city of Zagreb, the Medvednica Mountain is a popular destination for hiking and mountain climbing. The mountain is home to several trails that offer stunning views of the surrounding landscape, and there are a variety of routes available, ranging in difficulty from easy to challenging.

- **The Papuk Nature Park:** Located in eastern Croatia, the Papuk Nature Park is a beautiful natural park that is home to a variety of hiking and mountain-climbing trails. The park is known for its stunning views of the surrounding landscape and its diverse plant and animal life.

- **The Krka National Park:** Located in central Croatia, the Krka National Park is a beautiful natural park that is home to several hiking and mountain-climbing trails. The park is known for its stunning views of the surrounding landscape and its beautiful waterfalls.

- **The Mljet National Park:** Located on the island of Mljet, the Mljet National Park is a beautiful natural park that is home to several hiking and mountain-climbing trails. The park is known for its stunning views of the surrounding landscape and its beautiful beaches.

- **The Paklenica National Park:** Located on the Dalmatian coast, the Paklenica National Park is a beautiful natural park that is home to several hiking and mountain-climbing trails. The park is known for its stunning views of the surrounding landscape and its beautiful beaches.

- Skiing and snowboarding
- Croatia may not be the first place that comes to mind when thinking of skiing and snowboarding destinations, but the country has some ski resorts that offer a variety of winter sports activities. Here are some of the top ski resorts in Croatia:

- **The Sljeme Ski Resort:** Located near the city of Zagreb, the Sljeme Ski Resort is the largest and most popular ski resort in Croatia. The resort offers a variety of runs for skiers and snowboarders of all skill levels, as well as several other winter sports activities, such as snowshoeing and cross-country skiing.

- **The Kupres Ski Resort:** Located in the Dinaric Alps, the Kupres Ski Resort is a popular destination for skiers and snowboarders. The resort offers a variety of runs for skiers and snowboarders of all skill levels, as well as several other winter sports activities, such as snowshoeing and cross-country skiing.

- **The Platak Ski Resort:** Located near the city of Rijeka, the Platak Ski Resort is a popular destination for skiers and snowboarders. The resort offers a variety of runs for skiers and snowboarders of all skill levels, as well as several other winter sports activities, such as snowshoeing and cross-country skiing.

- **The Bjelolasica Ski Resort:** Located in the Lika region, the Bjelolasica Ski Resort is a popular destination for skiers and snowboarders. The resort offers a variety of runs for skiers and snowboarders of all skill levels, as well as several other winter sports activities, such as snowshoeing and cross-country skiing.

- **The Risnjak Ski Resort:** Located in the Gorski Kotar region, the Risnjak Ski Resort is a popular destination for skiers and snowboarders. The resort offers a variety of runs for skiers and snowboarders of all skill levels, as well as several other winter sports activities, such as snowshoeing and cross-country skiing.

- **The Mrkopalj Ski Resort:** Located in the Gorski Kotar region, the Mrkopalj Ski Resort is a popular destination for skiers and snowboarders. The resort offers a variety of runs for skiers and snowboarders of all skill levels, as well as several other winter sports activities, such as snowshoeing and cross-country skiing.

- **The Vransko Jezero Ski Resort:** Located in the Gorski Kotar region, the Vransko Jezero Ski Resort is a popular destination for skiers and snowboarders. The resort offers a variety of runs for skiers and snowboarders of all skill levels, as well as several other winter sports activities, such as snowshoeing and cross-country skiing.

- **The Samarske Stijene Ski Resort:** Located in the Gorski Kotar region, the Samarske Stijene Ski Resort is a popular destination for skiers and snowboarders. The resort offers a variety of runs for skiers and snowboarders of all skill levels, as well as several other winter sports activities, such as snowshoeing and cross-country skiing.

- **The Čelimbaša Ski Resort:** Located in the Gorski Kotar region, the Čelimbaša Ski Resort is a popular destination for skiers and snowboarders. The resort offers a variety of runs for skiers and snowboarders of all skill levels, as well as several other winter sports activities, such as snowshoeing and cross-country skiing.

- **The Bijela Stijena Ski Resort:** Located in the Gorski Kotar region, the Bijela Stijena Ski Resort is a popular destination for skiers and snowboarders. The resort offers a variety of runs for skiers and snowboarders of all skill levels, as well as several other winter sports activities, such as snowshoeing and cross-country skiing.

Beach And Water Sports

Croatia is a country with a stunning coastline and several beautiful beaches, making it a popular destination for beach and water sports enthusiasts. Here are some of the top destinations for beach and water sports in Croatia:

The Dubrovnik Riviera: Located on the Dalmatian coast, the Dubrovnik Riviera is known for its beautiful beaches and crystal-clear waters. The area is a popular destination for swimming, sunbathing, and a variety of water sports, including snorkeling, scuba diving, and sailing.

The Istrian Peninsula: Located on the Adriatic Sea, the Istrian Peninsula is known for its beautiful beaches and crystal-clear waters. The area is a popular destination for swimming, sunbathing, and a variety of water sports, including snorkeling, scuba diving, and sailing.

The Dalmatian Islands: Located off the coast of Croatia, the Dalmatian Islands are known for their beautiful beaches and crystal-clear waters. The islands are a popular destination for swimming, sunbathing, and a variety of water sports, including snorkeling, scuba diving, and sailing.

The Kvarner Gulf: Located on the Adriatic Sea, the Kvarner Gulf is known for its beautiful beaches and crystal-clear waters. The area is a popular destination for swimming, sunbathing, and a variety of water sports, including snorkeling, scuba diving, and sailing.

The Zadar Riviera: Located on the Dalmatian coast, the Zadar Riviera is known for its beautiful beaches and crystal-clear waters. The area is a popular destination for swimming, sunbathing, and a variety of water sports, including snorkeling, scuba diving, and sailing.

The Makarska Riviera: Located on the Dalmatian coast, the Makarska Riviera is known for its beautiful beaches and crystal-clear waters. The area is a popular destination for swimming, sunbathing, and a variety of water sports, including snorkeling, scuba diving, and sailing.

The Split Riviera: Located on the Dalmatian coast, the Split Riviera is known for its beautiful beaches and crystal-clear waters. The area is a popular destination for swimming, sunbathing, and a variety of water sports, including snorkeling, scuba diving, and sailing.

The Korčula Island: Located off the coast of Croatia, the Korčula Island is known for its beautiful beaches and crystal-clear waters. The island is a popular destination for swimming, sunbathing, and a variety of water sports, including snorkeling, scuba diving, and sailing.

The Cres Island: Located off the coast of Croatia, the Cres Island is known for its beautiful beaches and crystal-clear waters. The island is a popular destination for swimming, sunbathing, and a variety of water sports, including snorkeling, scuba diving, and sailing.

The Brač Island: Located off the coast of Croatia, the Brač Island is known for its beautiful beaches and crystal-clear waters. The island is a popular destination for swimming, sunbathing, and a variety of water sports, including snorkeling, scuba diving, and sailing.

Food And Drink

Restaurants And Cafes:

Croatia is a country with a diverse culinary scene, offering a variety of delicious dishes and drinks for visitors to enjoy. Here are some of the top restaurants and cafes in Croatia:

- **Konoba Dubrava:** Located in the city of Dubrovnik, Konoba Dubrava is a popular restaurant that serves traditional Croatian dishes made with fresh, local ingredients. The restaurant is known for its delicious seafood dishes, as well as its wine selection.

- **Konoba Bajamont:** Located in the city of Split, Konoba Bajamont is a popular restaurant that serves traditional Croatian dishes made with fresh, local ingredients. The restaurant is known for its delicious seafood dishes, as well as its wine selection.

- Nautika: Located in the city of Zagreb, Nautika is a popular restaurant that serves modern Croatian cuisine made with fresh, local ingredients. The restaurant is known for its delicious seafood dishes, as well as its wine selection.

- **Konoba Mate:** Located in the city of Rovinj, Konoba Mate is a popular restaurant that serves traditional Croatian dishes made with fresh, local ingredients. The restaurant is known for its delicious seafood dishes, as well as its wine selection.

- **Konoba Kod Joze:** Located in the town of Hvar, Konoba Kod Joze is a popular restaurant that serves traditional Croatian dishes made with fresh, local ingredients. The restaurant is known for its delicious seafood dishes, as well as its wine selection.

- **Konoba Didov San:** Located in the town of Cavtat, Konoba Didov San is a popular restaurant that serves traditional Croatian dishes made with fresh, local ingredients. The restaurant is known for its delicious seafood dishes, as well as its wine selection.

- **Konoba Nemo:** Located in the town of Omiš, Konoba Nemo is a popular restaurant that serves traditional Croatian dishes made with fresh, local ingredients. The restaurant is known for its delicious seafood dishes, as well as its wine selection.

- Konoba Pjat: Located in the town of Korčula, Konoba Pat is a popular restaurant that serves traditional Croatian dishes made with fresh, local ingredients. The restaurant is known for its delicious seafood dishes, as well as its wine selection.

- **Konoba Nono:** Located in the town of Šibenik, Konoba Nono is a popular restaurant that serves traditional Croatian dishes made with fresh, local ingredients. The restaurant is known for its delicious seafood dishes, as well as its wine selection.

- **Konoba Nacional:** Located in the city of Rijeka, Konoba Nacional is a popular restaurant that serves traditional Croatian dishes made with fresh, local ingredients. The restaurant is known for its delicious seafood dishes, as well as its wine selection.

Street Food And Markets:

Croatia is a country with a rich culinary culture, and there are several street food and markets throughout the country where visitors can try local dishes and purchase fresh, local ingredients. Here are some of the top street food and markets in Croatia:

- **The Zagreb Farmers' Market:** Located in the city of Zagreb, the Zagreb Farmers' Market is a popular destination for tourists and locals alike. The market is held every morning and is known for its fresh, local produce, as well as its selection of street food, including grilled meats, sandwiches, and pastries.

- **The Rijeka Fish Market:** Located in the city of Rijeka, the Rijeka Fish Market is a popular destination for tourists and locals alike. The market is known for its fresh, local seafood, as well as its selection of street food, including grilled seafood, sandwiches, and pastries.

- **The Split Green Market:** Located in the city of Split, the Split Green Market is a popular destination for tourists and locals alike. The market is known for its fresh, local produce, as well as its selection of street food, including grilled meats, sandwiches, and pastries.

- **The Dubrovnik Green Market:** Located in the city of Dubrovnik, the Dubrovnik Green Market is a popular destination for tourists and locals alike. The market is known for its fresh, local produce, as well as its selection of street food, including grilled meats, sandwiches, and pastries.

- **The Pula Market:** Located in the city of Pula, the Pula Market is a popular destination for tourists and locals alike. The market is known for its fresh, local produce, as well as its selection of street food, including grilled meats, sandwiches, and pastries.

- **The Zadar Green Market:** Located in the city of Zadar, the Zadar Green Market is a popular destination for tourists and locals alike. The market is known for its fresh, local produce, as well as its selection of street food, including grilled meats, sandwiches, and pastries.

- **The Šibenik Green Market:** Located in the city of Šibenik, the Šibenik Green Market is a popular destination for tourists and locals alike. The market is known for its fresh, local produce, as well as its selection of street food, including grilled meats, sandwiches, and pastries.

- **The Omiš Market:** Located in the town of Omiš, the Omiš Market is a popular destination for tourists and locals alike. The market is known for its fresh, local produce, as well as its selection of street food, including grilled meats, sandwiches, and pastries.

- **The Cavtat Market:** Located in the town of Cavtat, the Cavtat Market is a popular destination for tourists and locals alike. The market is known for its fresh, local produce, as well as its selection of street food, including grilled meats, sandwiches, and pastries.

- **The Korčula Market**: Located in the town of Korčula, the Korčula Market is a popular destination for tourists and locals alike. The market is known for its fresh, local produce, as well as its selection of street food, including grilled meats, sandwiches, and pastries.

Entertainment And Nightlife

Bars And Clubs

Croatia is a country with a vibrant nightlife scene, offering a variety of bars and clubs for visitors to enjoy. Here are some of the top bars and clubs in Croatia:

- **The Garden:** Located in the city of Zagreb, The Garden is a popular bar and club that features live music and DJs, as well as a variety of cocktails and beers.

- **The Open Air Club:** Located in the city of Split, The Open Air Club is a popular bar and club that features live music and DJs, as well as a variety of cocktails and beers.

- **The Club Fiume:** Located in the city of Rijeka, The Club Fiume is a popular bar and club that features live music and DJs, as well as a variety of cocktails and beers.

- **The Theatro Club:** Located in the city of Dubrovnik, The Theatro Club is a popular bar and club that features live music and DJs, as well as a variety of cocktails and beers.

- **The Hemingway Club:** Located in the city of Zagreb, The Hemingway Club is a popular bar and club that features live music and DJs, as well as a variety of cocktails and beers.

- These are just a few of the many bars and clubs that can be found in Croatia. Whether you're looking to dance the night away or simply enjoy a cocktail, there is something for everyone to enjoy in Croatia.

Theaters And Concerts:

there are many theaters and concert venues throughout the country where visitors can enjoy live performances. Here are some of the top theaters and concert venues in Croatia:

- **The Croatian National Theater:** Located in the city of Zagreb, the Croatian National Theater is the oldest and most prestigious theater in the country. The theater offers a variety of performances, including plays, operas, and ballets.

- **The Vatroslav Lisinski Concert:** Located in the city of Zagreb, the Vatroslav Lisinski Concert is a popular concert venue that hosts a variety of performances, including concerts, operas, and ballets.

- The Cro

- **atian National Theater in Split:** Located in the city of Split, the Croatian National Theater in Split is a popular theater that offers a variety of performances, including plays, operas, and ballets.

- **The Croatian National Theater in Rijeka:** Located in the city of Rijeka, the Croatian National Theater in Rijeka is a popular theater that offers a variety of performances, including plays, operas, and ballets.

- **The Croatian National Theater in Dubrovnik:** Located in the city of Dubrovnik, the Croatian National Theater in Dubrovnik is a popular theater that offers a variety of performances, including plays, operas, and ballets.

- **The Croatian National Theater in Osijek:** Located in the city of Osijek, the Croatian National Theater in Osijek is a popular theater that offers a variety of performances, including plays, operas, and ballets.

- **The Croatian National Theater in Varaždin:** Located in the city of Varaždin, the Croatian National Theater in Varaždin is a popular theater that offers a variety of performances, including plays, operas, and ballets.

- **The Croatian National Theater in Šibenik:** Located in the city of Šibenik, the Croatian National Theater in Šibenik is a popular theater that offers a variety of performances, including plays, operas, and ballets.

- **The Croatian National Theater in Pula:** Located in the city of Pula, the Croatian National Theater in Pula is a popular theater that offers a variety of performances, including plays, operas, and ballets.

- **The Croatian National Theater in Zadar:** Located in the city of Zadar, the Croatian National Theater in Zadar is a popular theater that offers a variety of performances, including plays, operas, and ballets.

Festivals And Events

there are many festivals and events held throughout the year that are popular with visitors. Here are some of the top festivals and events in Croatia:

- **The Dubrovnik Summer Festival:** Held annually in the city of Dubrovnik, the Dubrovnik

Summer Festival is a popular event that features a variety of performances, including concerts, plays, and operas. The festival runs from July to August and is held in various venues throughout the city.

- **The Split Summer Festival:** Held annually in the city of Split, the Split Summer Festival is a popular event that features a variety of performances, including concerts, plays, and operas. The festival runs from July to August and is held in various venues throughout the city.

- **The Pula Film Festival:** Held annually in the city of Pula, the Pula Film Festival is a popular event that showcases a selection of Croatian and international films. The festival runs from July to August and is held at the Pula Arena, a historic amphitheater.

- **The Zagreb Film Festival:** Held annually in the city of Zagreb, the Zagreb Film Festival is a popular event that showcases a selection of Croatian and international films. The festival runs from October to November and is held at various venues throughout the city.

- **The Ultra Europe Music Festival:** Held annually in the city of Split, the Ultra Europe Music Festival is a popular event that features a variety of electronic music acts. The festival runs in July and is held at the Poljud Stadium.

- **The INmusic Festival:** Held annually in the city of Zagreb, the INmusic Festival is a popular event that features a variety of music acts. The festival runs in June and is held at Jarun Lake.

-

- **The Dimensions Festival:** Held annually in the city of Pula, the Dimensions Festival is a popular event that features a variety of electronic music acts. The festival runs in August and is held at Fort Punta Christo.

- **The Outlook Festival:** Held annually in the city of Pula, the Outlook Festival is a popular event that features a variety of electronic music acts. The festival runs in September and is held at Fort Punta Christo.

- **The Rijeka Summer Nights:** Held annually in the city of Rijeka, the Rijeka Summer Nights is a popular event that features a variety of music acts. The festival runs from June to September and is held at various venues throughout the city.

- **The Umag Tennis Open:** Held annually in the town of Umag, the Umag Tennis Open is a popular event that features a variety of tennis matches. The tournament runs in July and is held at the Umag Tennis Academy.

CHAPTER 6: SHOPPING IN CROATIA

Department Stores And Malls

Croatia is a country with a thriving retail sector, offering a variety of department stores and malls for visitors to enjoy. These shopping centers provide a convenient one-stop shop for fashion, home goods, electronics, and more. Here are the top 10 department stores and malls in Croatia:

- **City Center One:** Located in the city of Zagreb, City Center One is the largest shopping mall in Croatia, with over 200 stores, including fashion, home goods, and electronics. The mall also features a food court with a variety of dining options and a cinema.

- **The Avenue Mall:** Located in the city of Zagreb, the Avenue Mall is a popular destination for shoppers, with over 100 stores, including fashion, home goods, and electronics. The mall also features a food court with a variety of dining options and a cinema.

- **The Mall of Split:** Located in the city of Split, the Mall of Split is a modern shopping center with over 100 stores, including fashion, home goods, and electronics. The mall also features a food court with a variety of dining options and a cinema.

- **The Super Nova:** Located in the city of Rijeka, the Super Nova is a popular department store that features a wide range of products, including fashion, home goods, and electronics. The store also has a food court and a cinema.

- **The Konzum:** Located throughout the country, Konzum is a popular grocery store chain that also sells a variety of home goods and electronics.

- **The Mercator:** Located throughout the country, Mercator is another popular grocery store chain that also sells a variety of home goods and electronics.

- **The City Center One East:** Located in the city of Zagreb, the City Center One East is a newer mall with over 100 stores, including fashion, home goods, and electronics. The mall also features a food court with a variety of dining options and a cinema.

- **The Kaptol Centar:** Located in the city of Zagreb, the Kaptol Centar is a popular mall with over 70 stores, including fashion, home goods, and electronics. The mall also features a food court with a variety of dining options and a cinema.

- **The Delta City:** Located in the city of Zagreb, Delta City is a modern shopping center with over

120 stores, including fashion, home goods, and electronics. The mall also features a food court with a variety of dining options and a cinema.

In addition to these department stores and malls, Croatia also has many smaller shopping centers and boutiques scattered throughout the country. These offer a more intimate shopping experience and often feature locally-made products and unique items. Whether you're looking for a convenient one-stop shop or a more personalized shopping experience, Croatia has something for everyone. So be sure to add some shopping to your itinerary on your next trip to the country.

Specialty Stores And Souvenir Shops

The Best Specialty Stores in Croatia for Foodies"

Croatia is known for its delicious cuisine, and there are many specialty stores throughout the country where foodies can find the best local ingredients and products. Some of the top specialty stores in Croatia for foodies include:

Oliva Gourmet in Zagreb: This specialty store offers a wide selection of high-quality olive oils, truffles, and other gourmet foods from all over Croatia.

Dubrovački Mlinovi in Dubrovnik: This specialty store is known for its fresh stone-ground flour and traditional Croatian kinds of pasta, as well as its selection of local olive oils and other gourmet foods.

Pekara Mlinar in Rijeka: This bakery is famous for its delicious pieces of bread, pastries, and other baked goods made with locally sourced ingredients. Zvijezda in Split: This specialty store is a must-visit for anyone interested in Croatian wine and spirits. They offer a wide selection of local wines, rakija's (fruit brandies), and other alcoholic beverages.

"Souvenir Shops In Croatia:

Where to Find the Best Gifts and Keepsakes"

Croatia is a popular vacation destination, and many visitors like to bring back souvenirs and gifts for friends and family. Some of the best souvenir shops in Croatia include:

- **Dubrovnik Gifts & Souvenirs:** Located in the heart of Dubrovnik's Old Town, this souvenir shop offers a wide selection of traditional Croatian gifts, including ceramics, jewelry, and textiles.

- **Croatian Gifts & Souvenirs in Split:** This souvenir shop is known for its selection of locally made crafts and gifts, including wooden carvings, pottery, and hand-painted glassware.

- **Rijeka Souvenirs:** This shop is located in the city center of Rijeka and offers a variety of souvenirs, including t-shirts, magnets, and other traditional Croatian gifts.

1. "The Best Specialty Stores in Croatia for Art and Craft Lovers"

Croatia is home to a thriving art and craft scene, and there are many specialty stores throughout the country where art and craft lovers can find unique and locally made products. Some of the top specialty stores in Croatia for art and craft lovers include:

- **Artisan Market in Zagreb:** This market, which is held every Sunday in Zagreb's Upper

Town, is a great place to find locally made crafts and artwork.

- Galerija Kolaž in Split: This gallery and shop feature a wide selection of contemporary Croatian art and crafts, including paintings, sculptures, and ceramics.

- **Dubrovnik Art Gallery:** Located in Dubrovnik's Old Town, this art gallery features a variety of locally made crafts and artwork, including paintings, sculptures, and jewelry.

2. "The Best Specialty Stores in Croatia for Fashion and Accessories"

Croatia is home to many talented fashion designers and artists, and there are many specialty stores throughout the country where fashion and accessory lovers can find unique and locally made products. Some of the top specialty stores in Croatia for fashion and accessories include:

- **Modi Atelier Elizabeta in Zagreb:** This boutique is known for its selection of high-quality, locally-made clothing and accessories.

- **Dubrovnik Fashion & Accessories:** Located in Dubrovnik's Old Town, this shop offers a wide selection of locally made fashion and accessory items, including bags, scarves, and jewelry.

- **Split Fashion & Accessories**: This shop is located in the city center of Split and offers a variety of locally made fashion and accessory items, including clothing, shoes, and handbags.

- **Rijeka Fashion & Accessories:** This shop, located in the city center of Rijeka, offers a wide selection of locally made fashion and accessory items, including clothing, jewelry, and scarves.

3. "The Best Specialty Stores in Croatia for Home Decor and Furniture"

Croatia is known for its rich history and cultural traditions, and there are many specialty stores throughout the country that offer unique and locally made home decor and furniture items. Some of the top specialty stores in Croatia for home decor and furniture include:

- **Dubrovnik Home Decor & Furniture:** Located in Dubrovnik's Old Town, this shop offers a wide selection of locally made home decor and furniture items, including pottery, textiles, and wooden furniture.

- **Rijeka Home Decor & Furniture:** This shop, located in the city center of Rijeka, offers a variety of locally made home decor and furniture items, including paintings, sculptures, and ceramics.

- **Split Home Decor & Furniture:** This shop, located in the city center of Split, offers a wide selection of locally made home decor and furniture items, including pottery, textiles, and wooden furniture.

6. "The Best Specialty Stores in Croatia for Books and Stationery"

Croatia has a thriving literary scene, and there are many specialty stores throughout the country that offer a wide selection of books and stationery items. Some of the top specialty stores in Croatia for books and stationery include:

- **Knjižara Čarobna Knjiga in Zagreb:** This bookstore, located in the city center of Zagreb, offers a wide selection of Croatian and international books, as well as a variety of stationery items.

- **Dubrovnik Books & Stationery:** Located in Dubrovnik's Old Town, this shop offers a wide selection of Croatian and international books, as well as a variety of stationery items.

- **Split Books & Stationery:** This shop, located in the city center of Split, offers a wide selection of Croatian and international books, as well as a variety of stationery items.

7. "The Best Specialty Stores in Croatia for Children's Toys and Games"

Croatia is home to many talented toy makers and game designers, and there are many specialty stores throughout the country that offer a wide selection of locally made children's toys and games. Some of the top specialty stores in Croatia for children's toys and games include:

- **Zagreb Toys & Games:** This shop, located in the city center of Zagreb, offers a wide selection of locally made children's toys and games, including dolls, stuffed animals, and board games.

- **Dubrovnik Toys & Games:** Located in Dubrovnik's Old Town, this shop offers a wide selection of locally made children's toys and games, including dolls, stuffed animals, and board games.

- **Split Toys & Games:** This shop, located in the city center of Split, offers a wide selection of locally made children's toys and games, including dolls, stuffed animals, and board games.

Markets And Street Vendors

1. The Best Markets in Croatia for Fresh Produce and Local Foods"

Croatia is known for its delicious cuisine, and there are many markets throughout the country where visitors can find fresh, locally-grown produce and other food products. Some of the top markets in Croatia for fresh produce and local foods include:

- **Dolac Market in Zagreb:** Located in the city center of Zagreb, this market is known for its selection of fresh produce, meats, cheeses, and other local foods.

- **Pazar in Dubrovnik:** This market, located just outside of Dubrovnik's Old Town, is a great place to find fresh fruits and vegetables, as well as local cheeses, meats, and other food products.

- **Rijeka Market:** This market, located in the city center of Rijeka, offers a wide selection of fresh produce, meats, cheeses, and other local foods.

2. "The Best Street Vendors in Croatia for Snacks and Street Food"

Croatia is home to many delicious street food options, and there are many street vendors throughout the country where visitors can try a variety of local snacks and meals. Some of the top street vendors in Croatia include:

- **Zagreb Street Food:** Located throughout the city center of Zagreb, these street vendors offer a variety of local snacks and street food, including grilled meats, sandwiches, and pastries.

- **Dubrovnik Street Food:** These street vendors, located throughout Dubrovnik's Old Town, offer a variety of local snacks and street food, including grilled meats, sandwiches, and pastries.

- **Rijeka Street Food:** These street vendors, located throughout the city center of Rijeka, offer a variety of local snacks and street food, including grilled meats, sandwiches, and pastries.

3. "The Best Markets in Croatia for Crafts and Souvenirs"

Croatia is home to many talented artisans and craftspeople, and there are many markets throughout the country where visitors can find locally made crafts and souvenirs. Some of the top markets in Croatia for crafts and souvenirs include:

- **Artisan Market in Zagreb:** This market, which is held every Sunday in Zagreb's Upper Town, is a great place to find locally made crafts and souvenirs, including ceramics, jewelry, and textiles.

- **Dubrovnik Crafts & Souvenirs:** These street vendors, located throughout Dubrovnik's Old Town, offer a variety of locally made crafts and souvenirs, including ceramics, jewelry, and textiles.

- **Split Crafts & Souvenirs:** These street vendors, located throughout the city center of Split, offer a variety of locally made crafts and souvenirs, including ceramics, jewelry, and textiles.

4. "The Best Street Vendors in Croatia for Clothing and Accessories"

Croatia is home to many talented fashion designers and artists, and there are many street vendors throughout the country where visitors can find locally made clothing and accessory items. Some of the top street vendors in Croatia for clothing and accessories include:

- **Zagreb Fashion & Accessories:** These street vendors, located throughout the city center of Zagreb, offer a variety of locally made clothing and accessory items, including bags, scarves, and jewelry.

- **Dubrovnik Fashion & Accessories:** These street vendors, located throughout Dubrovnik's Old Town, offer a variety of locally made clothing and accessory items, including bags, scarves, and jewelry.

- **Rijeka Fashion & Accessories:** These street vendors, located throughout the city center of Rijeka, offer a variety of locally made clothing and accessory items, including bags, scarves, and jewelry.

- **Split Fashion & Accessories:** These street vendors, located throughout the city center of Split, offer a variety of locally made clothing and accessory items, including bags, scarves, and jewelry.

Online Shopping And Delivery

Online shopping and delivery have become increasingly popular in Croatia in recent years, making it easier for consumers to purchase products and have them delivered to their doorstep. Here is a detailed overview of online shopping and delivery in Croatia:

"Popularity Of Online Shopping In Croatia"

According to a recent survey, around 75% of Croatian consumers have made an online purchases in the past year. This trend is expected to continue, as more and more Croatian consumers are turning to online shopping as a convenient and safe way to purchase products.

"Types of Products Available for Online Purchase in Croatia"

Consumers in Croatia can purchase a wide range of products online, including clothing, electronics, home goods, and more. Many Croatian retailers have an online presence, making it easy for consumers to shop for products from their favorite brands.

"Payment Options for Online Shopping in Croatia"
Croatian consumers can make online purchases using a variety of payment methods, including credit and debit cards, PayPal, and bank transfers. It is also common for Croatian retailers to offer cash on delivery (COD) as a payment option.

"Delivery Options for Online Purchases in Croatia"

Croatian retailers offer a variety of delivery options for online purchases, including standard delivery, express delivery, and pickup from a local store or pickup point. Delivery fees and times may vary depending on the retailer and the delivery option chosen.

"Online Shopping Safety and Security in Croatia"

Online shopping in Croatia is generally considered safe and secure, as Croatian retailers use secure payment systems and follow best practices for protecting consumer data. However, it is important for consumers to be cautious when shopping online and to only make purchases from reputable retailers.

"Growth of E-commerce in Croatia"

The e-commerce market in Croatia has seen significant growth in recent years, with online sales expected to continue to rise in the coming years. This trend is driven by the increasing popularity of online shopping among Croatian consumers and the expansion of e-commerce by Croatian retailers.

"Challenges and Opportunities for Online Retailers in Croatia"

One of the main challenges for online retailers in Croatia is the high level of competition, as more and more retailers enter the market. To stand out, retailers must offer a high-quality shopping experience and competitive prices. However, the growing popularity of online shopping in Croatia also presents opportunities for retailers, as there is increasing demand for online products and services.

online shopping and delivery in Croatia are convenient and popular options for consumers, offering a wide range of products and delivery options. While there are challenges for online retailers, the growing e-commerce market in Croatia also presents opportunities for businesses to reach and serve a larger customer base.

CHAPTER 7: TIPS AND CONSIDERATIONS FOR VISITING CROATIA

Etiquette And Customs

Etiquette and customs in Croatia are shaped by the country's history and cultural influences, including those from the Mediterranean region and Central Europe. Understanding and respecting these customs can help visitors to Croatia feel more welcome and enjoy their stay in the country.

Greetings And Social Norms

Greetings and social norms play an important role in Croatian culture and daily life. In this article, we will explore the various ways that Croatians greet one another, as well as the social norms and customs that are important to consider when interacting with people in Croatia.

Greetings in Croatia:

In Croatia, it is common to greet others with a handshake, a kiss on the cheek, or a hug. The type of greeting that is used depends on the relationship between the two people and the context in which the greeting takes place.

Handshakes are the most common greeting among men and are also appropriate for greeting women in a formal or professional setting. In more casual or friendly situations, it is common for men and women to greet each other with a kiss on the cheek.

This is done by leaning in and kissing the air near the other person's cheek, starting with the left cheek. It is important to note that this greeting is only appropriate between members of the same sex; men do not kiss women on the cheek, and women do not kiss men on the cheek.

Hugs are also a common greeting among friends and family members. In Croatia, it is common for people to hug each other when meeting after a long time apart or when expressing congratulations or congratulations.

It is important to remember that these greetings are not universal in Croatia, and it is always best to follow the lead of the person you are greeting. If you are unsure what to do, it is safe to start with a handshake and then observe the other person's reaction to see if a more familiar greeting is appropriate.

Social Norms In Croatia:

Croatian culture places a strong emphasis on social norms and customs, and it is important to be aware of these when interacting with people in Croatia. Here are a few social norms to consider:

- **Respect for authority:** In Croatia, it is important to show respect for authority, especially to elders and those in positions of power. This includes using formal titles and addressing people with the appropriate level of formality.

- **Personal space:** Croatians generally value their personal space and may feel uncomfortable if someone stands too close to them or touches them without permission. It is important to be aware of these boundaries and to respect them.

- **Dressing appropriately:** Croatians generally dress conservatively, especially in formal or professional settings. It is important to dress appropriately for the occasion and to avoid wearing clothing that is too revealing or casual.

- **Meals and dining:** Meals are an important part of Croatian culture, and there are a few social norms to consider when dining with Croatians. It is customary to wait for the host to sit down and begin eating before starting to eat yourself, and it is also common to wait for everyone at the table to be served before starting to eat. It is also considered rude to leave food on your plate, as it is seen as a sign that you were not satisfied with the meal.

Table Manners And Restaurant Etiquette:

Table manners and restaurant etiquette are an important part of Croatian culture and daily life. In this article, we will explore the various customs and norms that are important to consider when dining in Croatia.

Table Manners in Croatia:

Croatian culture places a strong emphasis on table manners, and it is important to be aware of these customs when dining with Croatians. Here are a few table manners to consider:

- **Wait to be seated:** In Croatia, it is common to wait for the host or hostess to show you your seat at the table.

- **Wait for the host to begin eating:** It is customary to wait for the host or hostess to sit down and begin eating before starting to eat yourself.

- **Use utensils appropriately:** Croatians generally use utensils to eat, and it is important to use them properly. This includes using a fork and knife to cut and eat food and using a spoon for soups and other liquids. It is also considered polite to keep your utensils in your dominant hand and to keep your knife on the right side of your plate and your fork on the left.

- **Don't leave food on your plate:** In Croatia, it is considered rude to leave food on your plate, as it is seen as a sign that you were not satisfied with the meal.

- **Use the "European" style of eating:** The "European" style of eating involves holding your fork in your dominant hand and using it to push food onto your spoon, which is held in your non-dominant hand. This is the preferred method of eating in Croatia, as opposed to the "American" style of using a fork and knife to cut and eat food.

Restaurant Etiquette In Croatia:

Dining out is an important part of Croatian culture, and there are a few customs and norms to consider when eating at a restaurant in Croatia:

- **Wait to be seated:** In Croatia, it is common for the host or hostess to show you to your table at a restaurant. It is also common for them to bring you a menu and ask if you would like anything to drink before taking your order.

- **Order and pay separately:** In Croatia, it is common for each person at the table to order and pay for their food and drink. It is also customary to leave a small tip (10-15%) for the waiter or waitress.

- **Use utensils appropriately:** As mentioned above, Croatians generally use utensils to eat, and it is important to use them properly when dining out.

- **Don't rush the meal:** In Croatia, meals are seen as a time to relax and enjoy the company of others, and it is not uncommon for people to spend several hours at a restaurant. It is important to take your time and enjoy the meal, rather than rushing through it.

Gift-giving and business cards

Gift-giving and business cards are an important part of Croatian culture and daily life, especially in business and professional settings. In this article, we will explore the various customs and norms related to gift-giving and business cards in Croatia.

Gift-Giving in Croatia:

Gift-giving is an important part of Croatian culture, and there are a few customs and norms to consider when giving gifts in Croatia:

- **Gifts for special occasions:** In Croatia, it is common to give gifts for special occasions such as birthdays, weddings, and holidays. It is also common to bring a small gift when visiting someone's home for the first time.

- **Gifts for business associates:** In a business setting, it is common to exchange small gifts as a way of showing appreciation or strengthening professional relationships. Gifts should be appropriate and not too extravagant, and it is important to consider the preferences and interests of the recipient.

- **Wrapping gifts:** In Croatia, it is common to wrap gifts in decorative paper or gift bags. It is also common to include a card or note with the gift.

Business Cards In Croatia:

Business cards are an important part of Croatian business culture, and there are a few customs and norms to consider when exchanging business cards in Croatia:

- **Use both hands:** When presenting or receiving a business card, it is considered polite to use both hands.

- **Treat business cards with respect:** In Croatia, business cards are seen as a representation of the person and their company, and it is important to treat them with respect. This includes not bending or writing on the card and presenting it in a clear and organized manner.

Exchange business cards at the beginning of a meeting: It is common to exchange business cards at the beginning of a business meeting or professional interaction in Croatia.

Health And Safety

Medical Care And Insurance:

Medical care and insurance are important considerations for anyone living or traveling in Croatia. In this article, we will explore the various options for medical care and insurance in Croatia, including the healthcare system, private insurance options, and emergency care.

The Healthcare System In Croatia:

Croatia has a universal healthcare system that is funded by the government and provides medical care to all Croatian citizens and legal residents. The system is based on a network of public hospitals, clinics, and primary care centers that are available to all citizens and legal residents.

To access the healthcare system, individuals must register with a primary care provider, who is responsible for coordinating their medical care. Primary care providers are usually general practitioner or a specialist in internal medicine, and they are responsible for coordinating the care of their patients with other healthcare professionals as needed.

Private Insurance Options In Croatia:

In addition to the public healthcare system, there are also private insurance options available in

Croatia. Private insurance can provide additional coverage for medical services that are not covered by the public healthcare system, such as private hospital rooms or specialized medical treatments. Private insurance can also provide faster access to medical care, as private hospitals and clinics often have shorter wait times than public facilities.

Private insurance is available to both Croatian citizens and foreign residents, and there are many private insurance companies to choose from. It is important to carefully research and compares the different options before choosing a private insurance policy.

Emergency Care In Croatia:

In the event of a medical emergency, individuals in Croatia can access emergency care by calling the emergency phone number 112. This number is available 24/7 and will connect you with the appropriate emergency services, such as ambulance, fire department, or police.

In addition to the emergency phone number, some several hospitals and clinics provide emergency care in Croatia. These facilities are equipped to handle a range of medical emergencies and are staffed by trained medical professionals.

Medical care and insurance are important considerations for anyone living or traveling in Croatia. The public healthcare system provides medical care to all Croatian citizens and legal residents, and there are also private insurance options available for those who want additional coverage. In the event of a medical emergency, individuals in Croatia can access emergency care by calling the emergency phone number or by visiting a hospital or clinic that provides emergency care.

Emergency services and contact information

Emergency services are an important resource in any country, and it is important to know how to access them in the event of an emergency. In this article, we will explore the various emergency services and contact information available in Croatia.

Emergency Services In Croatia:

In Croatia, there are several emergency services available to individuals in need of assistance, including:

Ambulance: The ambulance service in Croatia is responsible for providing medical care and transportation to individuals in need of emergency medical attention. The ambulance service can be accessed by calling the emergency phone number 112.

Fire department: The fire department in Croatia is responsible for responding to fires and other emergencies that require specialized equipment and expertise. The fire department can be accessed by calling the emergency phone number 112.

Police: The police in Croatia are responsible for maintaining public safety and order and can be contacted for emergencies or to report a crime. The police can be accessed by calling the emergency phone number 112.

Emergency Contact Information In Croatia:

In the event of an emergency in Croatia, it is important to know how to contact the appropriate emergency services. The emergency phone number 112 can be called from any phone and will connect you with the appropriate emergency service based on the nature of the emergency.

In addition to the emergency phone number, there are also a number of hospitals and clinics that provide emergency care in Croatia. These facilities are equipped to handle a range of medical emergencies and are staffed by trained medical professionals.

Emergency services are an important resource in Croatia, and it is important to know how to access them in the event of an emergency. The emergency phone number 112 can be called from any phone to connect you with the appropriate emergency service, and some several hospitals and clinics provide emergency care.

Respect For Local Culture

Dress code and clothing considerations

Dress code and clothing considerations are important to consider when living or traveling in Croatia. In this article, we will explore the various customs and norms related to dress codes and clothing in Croatia, including appropriate attire for different occasions and the influence of weather on clothing choices.

Dress Code in Croatia:

Croatian culture places a strong emphasis on dress code and appearance, and it is important to be aware of these customs when dressing in Croatia. Here are a few dress code considerations to keep in mind:

- **Formal occasions:** In Croatia, it is important to dress appropriately for formal occasions such as weddings, business meetings, and other events. For men, this typically means wearing a suit and tie, and for women, a formal dress or suit.

- **Casual occasions:** In more casual settings, it is acceptable to dress more casually, but it is still important to avoid clothing that is too revealing or casual.

- **Business dress code:** In a business setting, it is important to dress conservatively and professionally. For men, this typically means wearing a suit and tie, and for women, a business suit or professional attire.

Clothing Considerations In Croatia:

In addition to the dress code, there are also a few other clothing considerations to keep in mind when living or traveling in Croatia:

Weather: Croatia has a Mediterranean climate, with hot, dry summers and mild, wet winters. It is important to dress appropriately for the weather and to bring layers in the colder months.

1. **Cultural sensitivity:** It is important to be aware of cultural sensitivities when dressing in Croatia, and to avoid clothing that may be considered offensive or inappropriate.

2. **Comfort:** Croatia is a country with a rich cultural history and many interesting sites to visit, so it is important to dress comfortably to allow for exploring and sightseeing.

Dress code and clothing considerations are important to consider when living or traveling in Croatia. It is important to dress appropriately for the occasion and to be aware of cultural sensitivities and the influence of weather on clothing choices. By being mindful of these customs and norms, you can effectively communicate and interact with people in Croatia.

Public Behavior And Manners:

public behavior and manners in Croatia, including appropriate behavior in different settings and the importance of respect for authority and personal space.

Public Behavior in Croatia:

Croatian culture places a strong emphasis on public behavior and manners, and it is important to be aware of these customs when interacting with people in Croatia. Here are a few considerations to keep in mind:

- **Respect for authority:** In Croatia, it is important to show respect for authority, especially to elders and those in positions of power. This includes using formal titles and addressing people with the appropriate level of formality.

- **Personal space:** Croatians generally value their personal space and may feel uncomfortable if someone stands too close to them or touches them without permission. It is important to be aware of these boundaries and to respect them.

- **Public behavior:** In public settings, it is important to behave appropriately and to avoid disruptive or inappropriate behavior. This includes respecting the rules and regulations of public spaces and being mindful of others around you.

Manners In Croatia:

Manners are an important part of Croatian culture, and it is important to be aware of these customs when interacting with people in Croatia. Here are a few manners to consider:

- **Greetings:** In Croatia, it is common to greet others with a handshake, a kiss on the cheek, or a hug. The type of greeting that is used depends on the relationship between the two people and the context in which the greeting takes place.

- **Table manners:** Croatian culture places a strong emphasis on table manners, and it is important to be aware of these customs when dining with Croatians. This includes waiting for the host to begin eating, using utensils appropriately, and not leaving food on your plate.

- **Gifts:** Gift-giving is an important part of Croatian culture, and it is customary to bring a small gift when visiting someone's home for the first time. Gifts should be appropriate and not too extravagant, and it is important to consider the preferences and interests of the recipient.

CHAPTER 8: ADDITIONAL RESOURCES AND INFORMATION

Maps And Visitor Guides

Maps and visitor guides can be useful resources for anyone living or traveling in Croatia. Maps can help you navigate the country and find your way around different cities and towns, while visitor guides can provide information on local attractions, events, and other points of interest.

There are several maps and visitor guides available for Croatia, including online resources and print materials. Here are a few options to consider:

- **Online maps:** There are several online map resources available for Croatia, including Google Maps and MapQuest. These tools allow you to search for specific addresses or locations and can provide directions and other information about the area.

- **Print maps:** Print maps are available at tourist offices, bookstores, and other locations throughout Croatia. These maps can be useful for navigating the country and finding your way around different cities and towns.

- **Visitor guides:** Visitor guides are available in print and online, and provide information on local attractions, events, and other points of interest. They can be a useful resource for planning your trip and making the most of your time in Croatia.

It is important to note that maps and visitor guides may not always be up to date, and it is always a good idea to verify the information before relying on it. It is also a good idea to bring a map or GPS device with you when traveling in case you get lost or need to find your way to a specific location.

Printable Maps And Brochures:

There are several resources available for finding printable maps and brochures for Croatia. Some options include:

- **The Croatian National Tourist Board:** This organization provides a variety of resources, including printable maps, brochures, and guides to help you plan your trip to Croatia. You can find these resources on their website at https://www.croatia.hr/en-GB/experiences/travel-tools/brochures-and-maps.

- **Local tourist offices:** Many cities and towns in Croatia have their own tourist offices, which often provide maps and brochures to help visitors explore the area. You can find the location and contact information for these offices on the Croatian National Tourist Board's website.

- **Online map providers:** There are also several online map providers that offer printable maps of Croatia. Some options include Google Maps, MapQuest, and OpenStreetMap.

- **Travel guides:** Travel guides, such as Lonely Planet or Fodor's, often include maps and other resources for planning a trip to Croatia. You can find these guides in print or electronic format.

It's also worth noting that many hotels, hostels, and other accommodation providers in Croatia often provide maps and other information to help guests navigate the area. So if you're staying at a specific property, it's worth asking if they have any resources available.

Online Resources And App Recommendations:

Some many online resources and apps can be useful when planning a trip to Croatia or while you are traveling in the country. Some recommendations include:

- **The Croatian National Tourist Board website:** This website (https://www.croatia.hr/en-GB) is a great resource for planning a trip to Croatia. It provides information on destinations, activities, events, and more.

- **Google Maps:** Google Maps is a useful app for getting directions, finding attractions and restaurants, and getting an overall sense of the layout of a city or town.

- **TripAdvisor:** TripAdvisor is a popular travel website and app that allows users to find and book accommodations, restaurants, and activities. It also includes reviews and ratings from other travelers, which can help choose where to stay and what to do.

- **Local tourist offices:** Many cities and towns in Croatia have their own tourist offices, which often provide information and assistance to visitors. You can find the location and contact information for these offices on the Croatian National Tourist Board's website.

- **Offline maps:** It's always a good idea to have an offline map available when traveling, in case you don't have an internet connection. There are several apps that allow you to download maps for offline use, such as Maps. me or City Maps 2Go.

- **Transportation apps:** If you're planning on using public transportation during your trip to Croatia, it can be helpful to have a transportation app. The Croatian National Tourist Board website has a list of apps that provide information on bus, train, and ferry schedules, as well as ticket prices.

- **Language translation app:** If you don't speak Croatian, it can be helpful to have a language translation app on your phone. Some options include Google Translate or iTranslate.

- It's always a good idea to do some research and download any apps or resources that you think might be useful before your trip so that you have everything you need at your fingertips.

Contact Information For Tourist Information Centers

Here is a list of tourist information centers in Croatia:

1. Zagreb Tourist Board

Address: Trg bana Jelačića 10, 10000 Zagreb, Croatia

Phone: +385 1 4898 555

Email: info@infozagreb.hr

2. Dubrovnik Tourist Board

Address: Pile Gate, 10000 Dubrovnik, Croatia

Phone: +385 20 323 887

Email: info@tzdubrovnik.hr

3. Split Tourist Board

Address: Trg Republike 1, 21000 Split, Croatia

Phone: +385 21 348 600

Email: info@visitsplit.com

4. Rijeka Tourist Board

Address: Trg bana Jelačića 5, 51000 Rijeka, Croatia

Phone: +385 51 212 555

Email: info@tz-rijeka.hr

5. Poreč Tourist Board

Address: Pina Budicina 5, 52440 Poreč, Croatia

Phone: +385 52 452 080

Email: info@istria-porec.com

6. Zadar Tourist Board

Address: Obala hrvatske mornarice 4, 23000 Zadar,

Croatia

Phone: +385 23 316 166

Email: info@zadar.travel

7. Šibenik Tourist Board

Address: Trg Ivana Pavla II 3, 22000 Šibenik,

Croatia

Phone: +385 22 214 015

Email: info@sibenik-tourism.hr

8. Osijek Tourist Board

Address: Trg Ante Starčevića 7, 31000 Osijek, Croatia

Phone: +385 31 202 022

Email: info@tzosijek.hr

9. Varaždin Tourist Board

Address: Trg Kralja Tomislava 11, 42000 Varaždin, Croatia

Phone: +385 42 212 555

Email: info@tz-varazdin.hr

10. Karlovac Tourist Board

Address: Trg bana Josipa Jelačića 1, 47000 Karlovac, Croatia

Phone: +385 47 611 555

Email: info@karlovac-touristboard.hr

11. Crikvenica Tourist Board

Address: Selce bb, 51260 Crikvenica, Croatia

Phone: +385 51 241 111

Email: info@crikvenica.hr

12. Opatija Tourist Board

Address: Ulica maršala Tita 100, 51410 Opatija, Croatia

Phone: +385 51 271 111

Email: info@opatija-tourism.hr

13. Rovinj Tourist Board

Address: Grisia 7, 52210 Rovinj, Croatia

Phone: +385 52 811 566

Email: info@tzgrovinj.hr

14. Pula Tourist Board

Address: Foruma 5, 52100 Pula, Croatia

Phone: +385 52 219 800

Email: info@pulainfo.hr

15. Pazin Tourist Board

Address: Trg Svetog Trojstva 1, 52000 Pazin, Croatia

Phone: +385 52 624 801

Email: info@tz-pazin.hr

16. Novalja Tourist Board

Address: Trg republike 1, 53291 Novalja, Croatia

Phone: +385 53 661 111

Email: info@visitnovalja.com

17. Rabljena Tourist Board

Address: Trg kralja Tomislava 1, 51511 Rab, Croatia

Phone: +385 51 775 566

Email: info@rab.hr

18. Mali Lošinj Tourist Board

Address: Kralja Tomislava 5, 51550 Mali Lošinj, Croatia

Phone: +385 51 231 888

Email: info@tz-malilosinj.hr

19. Umag Tourist Board

Address: Trg slobode 3, 52470 Umag, Croatia

Phone: +385 52 757 011

Email: info@istra.hr

20. Vrsar Tourist Board

Address: Trg Maršala Tita 1, 52450 Vrsar, Croatia

Phone: +385 52 444 044

Email: info@istra.hr

Printed in Great Britain
by Amazon

17096124R00140